FV

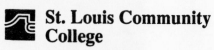

St. Louis Community College

Forest Park
Florissant Valley
Meramec

Instructional Resources
St. Louis, Missouri

GAYLORD

THE LAST GREAT AMERICAN HOBO

Photographs by Michael Williamson
Essay by Dale Maharidge

Prima Publishing

Production management: Bookman Productions
Book design: Brian Burch

Library of Congress Cataloging-in-Publication Data

Maharidge, Dale.
    The last great American hobo / Dale Maharidge and Michael
Williamson.
        p. cm.
    Includes index.
    ISBN 1-55958-299-5 : $21.95
    1. Tramps — United States.   I. Williamson, Michael.   II. Title.
HV4505.M34 1993   92-40480
305.5'68 — dc20   CIP

93 94 95 96 97 RRD 10 9 8 7 6 5 4 3 2 1
Printed in the United States of America

How to Order: Quantity discounts are available from Prima Publishing, P.O. Box 1260BK, Rocklin, CA 95677, telephone (916) 786-0426. On your letterhead, include information concerning the intended use of the books and the number of books you wish to purchase.

To all nonconformists, hobo and otherwise,
trampled by a society that exalts imitation rebels
but is intolerant of the real ones.

IN THE SUMMER OF 1989, Michael Williamson and I were troubled, for reasons then monumental but now rendered meaningless. We were employed by a newspaper, which was part of our trouble, and I was sitting in the newsroom one afternoon thinking about just how much trouble I was dealing with, when the telephone rang. It was a man I'll call Red. Red was a source who lived on the other side of the law across the river and knew all sorts of things. This time Red had information about an unsolved kidnap-homicide of two college sweethearts, a story I'd covered a decade earlier. Could we meet for lunch?

I crossed the Sacramento River into Broderick, where many citizens would have been pirates or Dust Bowl refugees in other eras. When we finished, Red asked if I'd been to Blackie's Camp. Red knew I had an interest in hobos and River People, for I'd first met him when he was a member of this community living among the weeds along the shore. He told me "Montana" Blackie was seventy-six years old and the greatest hobo he'd ever met.

Years earlier, Michael and I rode the rails for a book. We'd met many of the oldest hobos, whose road lives dated to the 1930s and early 1940s, guys such as No Thumbs, who patiently taught greenhorns like us the hobo ways and the hobo code. This code is not recorded in any traditional repository of our laws and morals but was etched in the collective consciousness of these men. It called for extending good manners to all decent people, to share, to respect railroad property so your fellow hobos are not made unwelcome, and to work when you can, among other things. Its ethos was a mix of the Golden Rule and being a proper gentleman. Its followers were members of a brotherhood.*

By the end of the 1980s, just about all of the old hobos had died off or quit the road. No Thumbs was murdered with two other hobos in a "thrill killing." There are plenty of replacements, given the decline of the American economy, but many younger hobos are of different breeding. The code has been dying with the veterans. Stupidly, I had never tape

---

Over the past ten years, Michael and I have ridden the rails many times, and we've never seen a woman or women traveling alone. Women usually accompany men. Hobo life is a very male lifestyle. There may be a solo woman hobo or two out there, but if they exist, they are rarities.

recorded their stories. We'd been searching in vain for any old timers who might be left. Meeting Blackie sounded like a final chance.

On that first visit, Blackie invited Red and me into his elaborate camp. He told fantastic stories. Again, I didn't have a tape recorder. I hurried back. I soon took Michael, who quickly outpaced my visits. He tells me his diary shows some 600 trips to the camp, plus his taking a two-week vacation there.

Blackie may have been the oldest active hobo left. We hesitate to proclaim him *the* oldest, for fear of some ninety-five-year-old hobbling out of the hobo jungle to dispute us, but we have been around and know of none. Blackie started riding the rails as a boy before the Depression, briefly in 1928, but he continued in the 1930s when hobos were generally seen as victims. He later resumed when the country was at the peak of its wealth, when he was seen as a romantic figure living outside the mainstream.

Then, in the 1980s, the streets were flooded with legions of homeless thousands, seen by many as a plague. Everywhere, the police began cracking down, from New York to San Francisco. These "sweeps" were news for a while, but they have become so common as to now be uncountable. At one antihomeless rally, Michael heard someone shout "homeless go home!" The word was get out of town, everywhere. Go anywhere but here.

Blackie was suddenly caught in a marching army of the dispossessed. He went from living an anonymous hobo life to running a gantlet. He'd been chased out of several towns. When Blackie came to the shore, he built his house, one of the finest shacks we'd ever seen, a veritable palace by tramp standards, complete with a water cooler, outhouse, oven. We thought it odd that he made such a grand house, when he could quickly lose it. But there was a reason, we later learned. Blackie was tired.

He didn't know it at the time, but Blackie had come to this shore to make a stand.

This book is a record of that stand. The bulk of events recorded here take place mostly over a fall, winter, and spring, on some 600 square feet of ground that encompassed his camp. It was a pivotal period for all involved: Blackie, Woody, Shorty, Luke, Herbert, Bill, Road Dog and Helga, Martin the steelworker, the mysterious woman, the authors, Vera, Alice and Burt and their pitbull Jaws, Moose the dog, Tie-Tie the other dog, Mister the cat, Harry the other hobo cat, not to be confused with Harry the rubber tramp who lived downstream in the green bus, the others. (A few names have been changed to keep the authorities from learning things, and I will not say which ones, but assume that the names of Mister and Moose are real, though don't be too certain about even this.)

"I'm going to Blackie's Camp" became a common thing for us to say. Blackie's Camp was a means of disappearing from our editors and the worries of our world, a mere two miles from our office. No matter the human situation, there is room for dignity, which was in plentiful supply at Blackie's Camp, as well as humor, which was even more abundant. Though we were still employed by a newspaper, we could never do a story while the camp existed. To publish anything about the camp would have been to destroy it, if not physically, then spiritually. It was our secret. Now that the round table is gone (Blackie's kitchen table was a giant wooden utility-wire spool turned on its side), its story can be told.

—Dale Maharidge
Palo Alto, California
October 21, 1992

CONTENTS

CONTENTS

Rolling down out of the north country into the top of California, the train crosses the lava beds, where no one lives and little grows. You gaze out the boxcar door at the rockbound earth jagged as fire-blackened glass, glad the train is hurrying through this land of dead volcanoes, because you want to get away from this empty place that makes you realize perfectly well what the terrible solitude of old age will be like. Or at least you think you know.

The train slows after Keddie, entering a forested canyon. It burrows through long tunnels, emerging to crawl across wooden bridges forty stories above a mountain river storming like snow through the gorge's granite dungeon. On a ledge above the whiteness lies the scattered carcass of a freight that plunged years ago. Looking down on the back of a raven soaring above the wreckage, you remember all the bad things they told you that can happen. You wonder how it felt for any hobos riding that train the moment a critical bridge timber gave out. The thought sends you reeling from the boxcar door, back to a dark corner.

When the train clears the canyon, it drops into the Central Valley, once again picking up speed. At the crossroads you see farmers behind the wheels of fatigued trucks, workers coming from jobs in lumbermills, professors from a community college. Some in the automobiles are oblivious to the *clang! clang! clang!* of the crossing gates, the screeches, the thump of a square wheel, the rush of wind. But others, the dreamers, carefully study the hundreds of tons of metal blurring past mist-spattered windshields. As long as the road and people who travel it have existed, there have been dreamers: some dream trains, others highways, still others rivers or the open sea. Hobos are just one kind of dreamer. These people in cars who look for them are another. A flash of recognition greets your presence in the fraction of an instant your eyes connect. A smile and a wave quickly follow from these citizens, who look on freights and the hobos who ride them as some do a ship on the ocean—a carrier of fantasies. Then the crossing gates lift, and they drive home and forget.

But as the sun goes down, you remember their faces as the flat country rolls by at sixty miles an hour and the cold sets in as frigid as the steel on which you are sitting. Lights come on in homes at the edge of the fields and orchards. Through the yellow window squares, you catch glimpses of the citizens eating dinner and watching television. Just before full darkness, the train goes past two boys playing on the siding, sons of Okies who have the same elongated bodies and narrow cave-cheeked faces of their fathers. They laugh as they throw stones at your boxcar, and you imagine one is saying "Gawd, I almost hit that bum!" but a near-miss isn't good enough and the wagered buck does not change hands.

The road that brought you to this valley is old. It was traveled by wanderers who came to this brown and sun-plagued state long before you were born, women with breasts sagging from the tugs of hungry babies, men with sparrow eyes fixed on shuffling feet. They're dead now, most of them, yet when the war drums of winter rain fall against the plywood shacks in the jungle camps, they say you can hear the lost cries of these broken men and women amid the wails of distant night trains. The oldest of the hobos still on the circuit remember their forebears: around the evening fire, the first sip wine does not pass through the lips of the living but is instead spilled on the earth to honor those now beneath it.

Not much has changed about this road and how it is traveled. The train you are on is out of Klamath Falls and before that Portland and before that Seattle, which is Big Nothin' country, as the Burlington Northern Railroad is known in the quarters you travel. You can catch the Big Nothin' into the cold immensity of Montana and the Dakotas, but you would never go any farther east, for Chicago is bad country for a hobo. All this is irrelevant, for you are heading south into the warm country, almost to Sacramento. If you catch a southbound hotshot there, you can be in Fresno in six hours, then go over the hump into Colton and Los Angeles, or veer off into the desert, to Needles, Yuma, or El Paso, the gateway to Juarez and old Mexico. Or you can go directly east, across the granite spine of the Sierra, into Reno, the Great Basin, Salt Lake City, beyond to Denver, the best of all hobo towns.

A train is a poem that will take you anywhere you want to go.

Though the train is better traveled, the river that comes into the Central Valley is no less poetic. The Sacramento River drains the whole of the northern and eastern interior of California. You can mark its origins in the mountains at the very top of the state and its conclusion at the Straits of Carquinez before it ultimately empties into San Francisco Bay. This river begins as a convergence of inconsequential creeks below the glacial snows of Mount Shasta and is just five miles old when it flows through Dunsmuir, a little mountain community that seems to have more Southern Pacific rail siding and interstate highway than town. If you know what you're doing, or at least know enough to have asked the old hobos camped by the K-Falls ice house, you'll take great care when coming into the Dunsmuir yard—before the train enters it, you'll hide to keep from being seen by the young bull. That railroad cop, known in every jungle up and down the circuit from K-Falls to Colton, has a reputation for pulling his gun and cracking heads.

The river and train are bound by the canyon at Dunsmuir, but the bond is broken below the town. The river takes a less serious course and is soon captured by Shasta Dam. Free of this encumbrance, it runs down a narrow valley, growing with the help of all the feeder branches to become a real river as the hills fall back and the land relaxes. Lodgepole and Jeffrey pines are replaced by tracts of almond, peach, and prune, which in the spring bloom form a cloud of pink and white across the vastness of the Central Valley. But in this season, the naked arms of the slumbering orchards often hide beneath the Tule fogs that can cover the whole of the Central Valley, more dense than mythical London fogs. These vapors arrive in December and sometimes last unbroken for several sunless weeks with the advance of that most disconsolate month in California's interior, closing in with the silence and finality of a country graveyard.

The levees confine the big river to its prehistoric and meandering course as it enters Sacramento—Spanish for the unleavened bread of the blessed sacrament, after which the river also takes its name. Here, the river once again meets with the train at the place where the Gold Rush pioneers first pitched tents in 1849 and talked of the wealth they expected to find in the mountains to the east. The river is wide and powerful, rushing past the low willow and cottonwood forest on the bank and the city lights beyond. The odor of smoky shore fires travels across the water. Figures gathered around the flames cast long shadows. The eyes of these men and women focus inward, on their campfires.

B LACKIE'S CAMP WAS SITUATED ON THE BANK OF THE SACRAMENTO RIVER, in the city of West Sacramento. The town was not always known by this geographically parasitic name—locals loyally call it Broderick, but the city fathers had big ideas when they incorporated the community into a city not long before Blackie arrived. The name change was supposed to improve upon the image of this town originally named after David Colbreth Broderick, who left a respectable job as a saloon owner to become a United States senator, a career change that ended in 1859 when he was the last public official in California to die in a duel.

Broderick is synonymous with "that part of town." It lies in an entirely different legal and cultural jurisdiction from the powerful city of Sacramento across the river, with its highrise office towers and the capitol building, where the business affairs of this populous state are conducted. It is certain that Broderick is poor. You will get no argument from many of those who live here. Big ideas have not yet changed the fact that Broderick is a place where those who never made it can, in their own way, make it.

A local industry is the strip of hotels inhabited by twenty-buck hookers. Most Broderickites can find little difference between them and the occupants of the state capitol across the river, except price, for to these people, the goings-on in that building are about as welcome and distant to their lives as events that occur in the Kremlin. While some occupants of that domed building sometimes journey across the Tower Bridge that links the communities to visit the women in the hotels, indulging in what could be deemed a redistribution of wealth, few Broderick citizens ever venture across the bridge. Everything they need exists here, including entertainment in the form of Saturday night brawls in the pool hall and numerous bars. These fights, carried on if not in the name, then in the spirit of Senator Broderick, can be spectacular in their magnitude.

The streets of Broderick are lined with ash trees, a substandard breed of that species that was the cheapest to plant back in the days when the town was settled. Such a choice was consistent with the fact that Broderick never had the best or even a middling of anything, only what no one else would take. This type of ash is particularly susceptible to infestations of mistletoe, an evergreen parasite that grows in the limbs and that has leached the trees into a state of near death. On these streets are homes also close to their own form of death. They display abandoned refrigerators and overstuffed, torn living-room chairs set on the porches, cracked window glass replaced with cardboard, and rusted screen doors worn at the spot above the doorknob where a patina of dirt shines from many years of use by the gripping hands of the poor. These are considered the finer homes of Broderick, many steps above the neighborhoods of one-room shacks, now extinct, demolished in the interest of the urban renewal that accompanied the changing of the town's name. They were set in clusters so compact that some of the shacks that had begun leaning from age rested against others of their kind, and it was clear this was the support that kept them from tumbling. These whitewashed shacks were cheaply rented by old men destined to die alone and unclaimed. Nearby are the trailer courts, into which passed successive generations of migrant workers, white, black, and brown, who have never succeeded by conventional standards, outcast from prosperous members of their races.

Closest to the river are the bushes and weeds that were home to the dwellers of the shore, a class of men and women polite society prefers to term *homeless*. Others call them *bums* and *whores* with no small amount of contempt. There are those who believe people study for such an existence in the way some work to become doctors or lawyers, living their lives in a fine-tuned series of steadily degenerating wrong turns that bring them to this level.

All this is a matter of perspective and is irrelevant to the people being called these things. Those who live on the shore have no labels for themselves, other than *River People,* for to be in a position to affix such labels to yourself or others, you have to be well off both financially and in other ways to afford the luxury of such contemplation.

River People were afforded a relatively high degree of respect by the citizens of Broderick, for a fair number had themselves lived on the bank at one time or another, or, if they had not, seemed on the verge of such a fate. A miscalculation of the rent money, a drunken binge at the wrong time of month, a fight with a spouse or boss, an improperly completed welfare form—any of these things could send them over the edge, busted and on the shore.

Blackie's Camp was located in the epicenter of the loose-knit community of River People that had swollen in number not long before we showed up. There had been a mass exodus from the Sacramento side of the river, first due to the predations of a renegade police officer known to River People as *Bronco Billy,* after the type of vehicle he drove, later due to officially sanctioned police sweeps. The west bank had long been a safe haven of sorts. It was patrolled by the sheriff of Yolo County before Broderick was incorporated by the men with ideas, and there was little concern for bothering River People. The police of the newly incorporated city of West Sacramento had not yet changed that policy.

The route to Blackie's Camp was to cross the Tower Bridge over the Sacramento River. You took the first exit, looping beneath the underpass, and came up in front of a rice mill. Going behind the mill, you went through an abandoned crash test site on a dusty lane that tried the suspension of the best car. On the left was a trailer belonging to Fanny the prostitute. Beyond was a cluster of bamboo, where some men who have no bearing on this story lived. Next was a turnoff that went down the levee to Blackie's Camp. It was not advisable to drive over this steep bank, but to park on top of the levee directly behind the rice mill's elevators.

The camp was not visible through the thickness of the trees on the sloping levee. But through breaks, there was a clear view of the broad river. If the hour was sunset, the river was the color of a poorly polished kettle; I imagine it was the same at dawn, an hour I never visited the camp. At other times of day the river was the silver of an old weathered shack. The river was perfectly calm when the tide was coming in. (The river is only a few feet above sea level.) If the tide was going out, the river was fast and could be heard, powerful as the Mississippi.

The air was always occupied with other sounds: water crashing from a sewer plant outfall across the river and the round-the-clock grinding of the rice mill as it processed grain freshly harvested from the vast paddies that cover the Sacramento Valley upriver.

Blackie's Camp materialized when you walked down the sandy path. But to call it a camp does a disservice, for this implies an accidental collection of tents of the tourist variety, hastily erected and without thought of permanence. It was actually a small city consisting of two main houses, several tents, a camper shell, and an abandoned car.

Blackie's house dominated the little community built on the bank just above the high-water line. It was set to exactly face the rising sun, about the size of an ordinary bedroom, and it took just two days to build. The only thing Blackie had to purchase was a $16 rain tarp to place over the flat sloping roof. Nails were salvaged from a load of dumped sheetrock. Plywood and two-by-fours were magically procured, and cardboard paneled the inner walls. It even had a door on hinges, a window (a sheet of plastic), a built-in bed with a mattress, candles for light, and a library shelf. It smelled like a house of great age, the kind you find in the American South, where the humidity and the odors of time impart a must like that of wet things never fully dried. There was a nightstand that contained an ashtray, a fishing reel, a transistor radio. Beneath the nightstand was a broken hedge trimmer with one sharp blade, at the ready for intruders. On the wall opposite the bed was a very pink three-foot picture of "Sherrie, tart of the year," turned upside down so that a standing man was at eye level with her best parts.

But this does not fully describe what grew from humble beginnings. The camp expanded beyond the main house itself, to include a porch, a fire ring in front of the porch that was the center of all social activity, an outhouse, a water cooler, and a cooking fireplace (separate from the fire ring) with an oven of sorts, made of square blocks of cement, built to table height. A piece of quarter-inch plate steel held the coals, and a dismantled shopping cart formed a grate. A pot of coffee, carbonized on the exterior to match the overcooked contents, usually perked atop this grill. Blackie had nailed a board between two cottonwoods behind the grill, and from it hung seven skillets. Other kitchen utensils were suspended from the rafters of the porch that nearly extended to the fireplace. The chairs were salvaged from the riverbank or plucked from abandoned cars. The earth, packed like asphalt, bore the frequent workings of a rake and broom. The giant wooden utility-wire spool, as mentioned, was the table, covered with a flower-pattern cloth. In the center, a pony-size Miller beer bottle was reincarnated as a salt shaker, the cap punched with holes.

This is what I saw that first time Red took me to see Blackie and what I came to discover over the coming months. The camp was a marvel, for I'd been at the shore back in June (some five weeks earlier, when I first met Alice and Burt, who lived in a camp just to the north) and almost none of it had existed. I recall there had been a truck camper, which was still to the south; it belonged to Bill, Blackie's traveling partner for the past three years. Where Blackie's house stood, there had only been a piece of plastic strung between two trees. There had been nothing on the site of the second dwelling, home to Herbert, a man from Texas and the only permanent nonhobo member of the camp.

That first day, Blackie was sitting at the round table beneath his porch. Blackie hollered a friendly hello. He had a beard crazy as a field of star thistle, its whiteness marred by a yellow circle around his mouth, either stained from tobacco or torched by errant matches that lit the hand-rolled cigarettes he smoked. He struck me as a combination of New England sea captain—based on appearance and hardscrabble language—and leprechaun, because of the way he moved.

"This river is for would bes and has beens," Blackie announced in a voice that had a hint of a Boston accent. "There's hippie-dippies, winos, and dingbats. I've been on the road since 1928, off and on. That's my life. I don't want to be doing anything else."

I remember he had maybe a thirty-inch waist and he moved fast. He got up and kicked the air several times when making a point. He seemed much younger than a man approaching four score in age. We talked for an hour. The conversation grew animated when I found he knew many of the old hobos we'd once run into or had heard of, now all dead, guys like No Thumbs, Mountain Dew, Hunchback Jack.

Blackie talked of hobos and citizens, the latter used to refer to nonhobos who lived in regular houses, said in the third person, as one might refer to residents of a foreign country. The nearest citizens were quite some distance away, but they were just Broderick people who lived in houses that weren't really much better than Blackie's shack. Things were changing, though. Within shouting distance to the north, across the avenue, was a huge construction project ready to start in a matter of a few months.

"That's supposed to be worth $300 million," Blackie said of the project that included a hotel and condominiums, the dream of a local businessman who owned a supermarket chain. This businessman did not know it, but he provided the camp's fireplace grill—Blackie used one of the chain's carts to make it.

"Thanks to Mr. ['X'] for this," Blackie said, pointing to the fireplace. "He's gonna start [the project] the first of the year. Even the Japanese are involved. Supposed to be a 650-room hotel right there. Six hundred and fifty rooms, brother."

Blackie said the waterfront condominiums were supposed to go for a half million dollars—he noted he now had the same view of the river they were going to have, but that he had it for free.

I came back in a few days, and Blackie was sitting at the round table. We were alone this time. He poured us coffee from the pot on the grill.

"I didn't think I'd get away with this. It's great, brother. Shit, look at that thing on there, sixteen bucks worth of tarp," he said, pointing to his house, his face filled with admiration for his work and the pride that he had built it for nearly free.

"After it turns out, I found a roll of tar paper that thick," he said of the material he could have used to waterproof the roof. "Ain't that a bitch?"

I asked if it was the best camp he'd ever had in all his years on the road.

"Hell no, Christ, I had camps in Minnesota, North Dakota, all over hell." He told me they were more grand than this, though he said this house had much in common with the classic Depression-era shacks of his early hobo life.

"You've got to maintain, keep your camp clean. Son'bitch can't keep his camp clean, he's no good. Well, I figure I might be on the fucking road, a dirty old filthy bastard, but my place is going to be clean. The old hobos in the old days, they used to be a bindlestiff, that bastard packed everything, and if he was crazy, he had a name for every pot and pan hung on the fucking wire of his tree. The old bindlestiffs are gone. A few around like myself. There's only a few crazy diehard bastards like me around that still motivate.* As far as hoboin' goes, it's the same as it used to be. Fuck the idea of steam trains. All they did was change the motivation, that's all. There ain't a damn thing modernized. Still the same old tracks. Same units. Same goddamn road, clickity-clack on down the line. Really nothin' has changed over the years, not for me anyway."

He did allow some changes.

"See back in the days I started riding, I used to ride the rods. Rods come underneath, supported the car. What you do is grab old pilings, or two-by-eights, put 'em across there, roll out, go to sleep. Once in a while, the train's liable to hit a fucking rock that bounces up and smacks you, ya' know. Oh, what the hell, inconvenience of the road. Jesus Christ, there ain't no rods. Used to be wooden boxcars, now they're all steel. On passengers, when I wanted to go fast, I rode the steps. Where they put the steel plate down, you know, I go over there, go up underneath there, see, then when the train gets motivating, it gets raised up, there you are, inside the fucking car. You wait ten, fifteen minutes, see the conductor go through, collecting tickets, you walk on in, flop your ass down."

Amtrak passenger trains afford no such opportunities for modern hobos. Freight trains, however, still have plenty of nooks. While railroads officially frown on hobos, there is a large degree of tolerance among workers that allows hobos to ride flat cars, boxcars, grain cars—yard workers are usually quite helpful to hobos. But there is a strict rule even among the workers that no ordinary hobo rides the engines, known as *units*. On a big train, there can be five units, the last four of which are unoccupied. With his becoming a senior member of hobo society, Blackie has found a few perks.

"Now, I ride the units a lot. Fuck yeah, cold up in Oregon, Washington, Montana, I ride them units. Nine times out of ten, the engineers know me, they say get in that last unit, we didn't see ya'. Sit on the iron floor, roll out my bedroll. When it gets moving, reach over there and turn on the fucking wall heaters. Need hot water, there it is, right there. Shithouse right there, what more do I want? Fucking first class."

The bulls are another matter. Even many workers don't like the bulls, who are railroad police with arrest powers. The bulls do not ride the trains but work in the railyards. For some reason,

---

* Blackie used the word "motivate" to mean an individual riding the rails, apparently a derivative of "motive power," as opposed to spiritual inspiration, though riding a train can spiritually inspire a hobo.

the vehicles they drive are almost always painted white. Like all hobos in the know, Blackie hid from the Dunsmuir bull, but he'd come across some who weren't so bad. Blackie liked Roger, an old bull who worked for the Southern Pacific in Klamath Falls. (Roger caught Michael and me a decade earlier on our first hobo trip, then told us on which track and at what time the next southbound was due.) But that fellow had since retired.

"Fact is, the bulls were a little tougher back then," Blackie said, as were the train workers. "Back then, they wanted fucking money to ride. You didn't have money, they kicked your fucking ass off. The brakie come back one time, walking on top of the fucking cars, looking for money. He come up to us and said you got any money? We ain't got none. Get the fuck off. Give him a buck or two, he didn't care.

"Other 'bos tell me a town is hot. Hell, I love to go to that town and harass the fucking railroad bull, give him a hard way to go. 'Specially up in Havre, Montana, that fucking bull up there. He fucks with me all the time. All they do is take your name down, social security, put your ass on the computer. They say the next time we see ya', you're going to jail. He might see you twenty times. They don't want to put you in jail. The railroad is not going to put out fifty bucks a day to keep your ass in jail for ten days. It's like Lincoln, Nebraska. What am I doin'? Sittin' back on my ass waitin' for a train to Kansas City. They wrote me up there for criminal trespass on railroad property. He writes me out a fucking ticket and I wiped my butthole with it and that was the end of it."

As for hobos, there had been great change in the nature of his younger brethren, but Blackie did not romanticize the bindlestiffs of the 1930s. Then, as now, there were *streamliners,* a hobo term for guys who'd come into the jungles with little or no gear, intent on stealing. I told Blackie that ten years earlier, Michael and I had run into a streamliner who nearly got us arrested when he was messing around in a nearby caboose at the Denver, Rio Grande & Western yard in Salt Lake City. He had nothing. When we ran into the same man one day later in Grand Junction, he had backpack and bedroll.

"You got to watch them suckers. You'll stick your shit over somewhere and think there ain't a swingin' dick around for miles, and you'll walk up town, get your little groceries, your little drink, whatever you want, and c'mon back, find your shit gone."

Hobos borrow a cliché applicable to their world—what goes around, comes around. You repeatedly see the same people as you ride the circuit, Blackie said, and eventually you'll run into the man who ripped you off. Blackie said thieves don't last.

"You put the word on him. The word on the road flies so fucking fast. It's here now, and it'll be in Seattle tonight. Somebody will punch him out, kick his ass."

In the old days, veteran hobos taught new guys; this was viewed as a duty, for the veterans had long ago been broken in by those who came before them. Nowadays, younger hobos often have an every-man-for-himself attitude. Blackie, however, kept the old code alive. His latest protégé was his campmate Herbert.

"Teaching him the hobo's life. He's getting to know it pretty good. Learning how to Dumpster dive, pick up cans. He likes it. Workin' son'bitch, too. Hardest thing in the world is to break somebody new into the tracks, break him into a camp. Learn him how to get the goddamn wood, how to get the water, wash the dishes. You teach the guy the ropes: where to score, where not to score, what to do, what not to do. And no goddamn shoplifting and thievery in between."

Blackie's camp was for hobos or hobos in training. He made the mistake of allowing in some *homeguards,* the hobo name for wastrels who don't travel; these used to be called *winos* by the general citizenry in pre–politically correct times.

"I got a couple of people 'round here that ain't hobos. This is where I let those guys sleep," Blackie said, pointing to a few tents at the camp's edge. "But that's got to go. This morning I give them the word to get the fuck out. I don't know if it's gonna work or not. I need hobos here. These guys just want to suck wine and fall over. Fuck 'em, I don't need 'em. Fuck that homeguard mother fucker. It's a big river. Find somewhere else. It's me, my generosity. I let 'em sleep here."

B LACKIE TOLD DOZENS OF STORIES WHILE SITTING AT THE CAMPFIRE or the round table those first weeks. Blackie was happiest when he was telling yarns, which he had in bottomless supply.

THE ALPO KIDS

"The Alpo kids. I left over here from Roseville, went up to K-Falls, bailed off, and they called me over and asked me if I wanted something to eat. I was hungry. Comin' up over the hump was cold, you know, comin' outta Dunsmuir. Anyway, they said look at that stew. Man it looks good. I said yeah, okay, so I make the store and come back and they're fixen to catch up the SP to Eugene, you see. Me, I'm goin' to Bend. So I look at this fucking stew, and say it looks pretty good and go at it. So I get up an' have a piss call, walk over by the fence an' see these fresh fucking Alpo cans. I scratched my head and said these guys don't have a dog, you know. So I go back and I grab a chunk of that meat and I break it open. Horse meat. Alpo dog food is what they eat, see. They added vegetables to it. So, the next morning, Bigger George comes by, him and Big Ernie and this other guy. They say whattya got, what's happenin'. I say there's the stew there, heat it up an' cook it. Old Bigger George had the shit running down his jaws. You oughta see that mother.

"I caught up with the friks near Spokane, an' they said, 'oh Blackie, don't say nuthin'. We've been eatin' that off'n on for twelve years.' Eatin' Alpo. They said don't tell nobody. They're still around.

THE FRISCO CIRCLE AND THE LUMP

"The Frisco circle. You draw a circle in the dust. Everybody chips in a dime, quarter, anything of value that you can hock or sell it, and you take it to get wine, food, whatever, that's the way it used to be.

"See back in the old days, for instance, I'm gonna tell you one little story. This is back around '36. We're sittin' in Stockton—you been to Stockton?—between the WP and the SP in the gully, that used to be the jungle, all the fruit tramps and everybody else was right there. All right, so one morning, we're sitting around there, made a Frisco circle, an' got enough for two half gallons. In those days, Tokay was number one. Never heard of Twenty-Twenty or none of that crap. Tokay was it, either White Port or Dark Port. That was your fortified crap.

"I told Montana Red, tell you what, mother fucker, I'll get a bigger fucking lump than you can today. What I mean by lump is go over and panhandle that fucking house, go to work for them, whatnot, rake the yard, and I says I got five bucks that says you can't, son'bitch. There was eight of us. So five bucks apiece goes into the pot, and old Peg Leg Pete, a one-legged mother fucker, he puts a big old stomper on it. Well, he says, pick out your house. There was eight of us, and old Peg Leg was our camp cook. So's I said, I'll take that one right there. An old shitty gray-lookin' house there, so they laughed at me an' said that thing's probably been bummed to death.

"See, back in the old days, houses were marked. Good was one X. Two XXs was fair. Three XXXs, no fucking way. They had other marks they put on buildings. They said bad dog, good dog, you get a little work here. You just put an X outside the door. They might give you a little bit of dried coffee, a little bit of sugar, some bread, or whatnot, good for a sandwich or two. Anyway, this fucking house I got to, I walk in, and the old lady is out in the yard. I said, 'morning ma'am.' The woman was about fifty-some years old. She put her roses in her apron and says, 'what can I do for you?' I said look here, I'm one of these hobos over there. She says yeah, I see you guys all the time. I said you need that yard worked on, rake up the yard or something? She says, I've lived here eighteen years and you're the first hobo ever to come to my door. She said you sit right here, I have something for you.

"Son of a bitch, what does she do? She outdoes herself. By the time she calls me in the kitchen, you know, I looked through the screen door and I likely got sick. On the kitchen table is five big boxes of shit. You name it brother, it was there. The old lady was a miser. She had cans of peas, cans of corn, all dried stuff, everything available, you name the shit, it's all in these boxes. I say, why you getting rid of all this? She said, well, it's been here for years, and some of the canned goods is dated back a few years, peaches and pears, string beans and so forth. I looked at this, you know, I'll need a cart to haul all this shit back. I said I know, I'll take it outside the fence and holler for them fuckers over there. I see them coming back carrying little bags. Here I got five boxes of shit, brother. That's the way us hobos used to do it in the old days."

CHICKEN LEG

"I want to tell you a good one. I bailed off a freight in Lincoln, Nebraska. Nickel Plate Road, which is no more. I bailed off that son'bitch by the bridge by the river. The reason I went to Lincoln was to make some money. There was about eight to ten tramps over there by the bridges, see. They spotted me. Hey Blackie, get your ass down here. Got a drink. Trucked on down. Drink the *Muscadoodle,* you know, Muscatel. I take a big swig of that. They say, where you headed for? I say uptown, man. I ask them to watch my gear. I truck uptown, it's daylight you know, took care of my business, got my bottle, come on back, got a half gallon for the camp, plus my fifth of whiskey, so they say are you hungry? I say I can always eat. He says there's a five-gallon bucket of stew over there, you know. All right. Raise the old wooden lid they had on top of it. Fucking chicken. Chicken and dumplings. I got me a pound coffee can, bring the fork outta my back pocket, start digging in there, and it's nothing but thighs and drumsticks. What the hell kinda pot's this? I get three big pieces of chicken, a bunch of dumplings, a big piece of hunky bread, bohunk bread, sit over there, they got hot peppers, so I'm eatin'.

"A little later on, they run out of juice, so they got to go before the store closes. So, these two guys take off and make a run, made a Frisco circle, and I threw in a buck or so. Guy says you feel like makin' a little run with me? That express is in now, and I got to hit it. This is a hot shot. So we go on up there and check it out. Back then they had the cattle cars, haul hogs and cattle. Now they don't do that shit no more. Walking down there, fucking chickens. He had a space about that much, you know, narrow. He reaches in his coat and gets a clothes hanger, bends the fucking wire, and he's got him a burlap sack, an old gunny sack. Reaches up through there, puts the wire around a chicken's leg, gives it a jerk, and here come the goddamn leg and all off. Hear the chicken in there dying. That's what I was telling you about the pot. That's how come it was full of thighs and drumsticks. That guy was a raunchy mother fucker. Takes the legs and puts them in the sack, feathers and all, takes them home and plucks them. And throws them in the fucking pot."

Usually, it was just Michael and I, or perhaps Red, who heard these stories. Bill and Herbert would drift away when we showed up. They didn't want us to know them, and that was okay. There was nothing awkward about this—that's just the way it was.

Blackie smoked while he talked. He rolled his own cigarettes on a little machine made for the purpose.

"Save a lot of bucks for a fucker who chain smokes, brother."

Blackie said his hobo name came from a job in Montana.

"I was working in a graphite mine, and I worked the buckets hauling the ore in and out of the shaft. Had a colored dude running the shovel. When we was takin' a shower, he said, 'hey, I got a new name for you'—he was always fucking with people—'we're gonna call you Montana Blackie.' The only thing white was here," he said, holding his rounded fingers around his eyes, "where I got my goggles, see, and the rest was black. It stuck."

His first hobo ride was in 1928, from Santa Barbara, where he lived, to Los Angeles.

"I was about thirteen then. We got a bug in our ass, got tired of Santa Barbara. There was two of us, me and this other young guy . . . he's a doctor today. He's retired. We hit the fucking road runnin' with 'bos. They treated us right, we treated them right. We could always pick up a telephone and call home and get money."

He went back home, but he hit the rails for real in the 1930s.

"Oh hell, nobody had a damn thing in the thirties. A lot of 'em worked the WPA.* A lot of 'em become fruit tramps, if you know what I mean, worked the apples, pickin', all the other stuff. Now that's passed, it only lasts about twenty-eight days, then the apple season's over. They got potato machines and fuckin' tomato machines, everything's all automated. Back in the thirties when Two Street was here you had labor contractors, and they'd take you out, down to Firebaugh, picking cotton. I never went in for that shit. Construction, that's my occupation, plumbing and electrical. I can make more accidentally than these fuckers out there working fourteen hours a day, chopping these fucking sugar beets. I'd starve ta' death first. The time you do all day, whattya got, about four dollars? Work all day for four fucking dollars."

After the Depression, Blackie told us he rode off and on again over the next few decades, with time out for service in World War II and Korea and for being married.

Historically, new hobos have been created in large numbers following wars and depressions. After the Civil War, an army of job seekers hit the rails that were then spanning the country. They carried hoes to do farm work, making them "hoe boys," or so one story goes. They would tie their goods in a bindle on the end of the hoe—this was in the days before aluminum-frame backpacks—and this is the basis of the classic cartoon image of a hobo carrying everything he owns at the end of a stick. But the exact root of the word *hobo* is lost. Another story has it coming from the word *gypoes,* a variation of *gypsy.* The word *hobo* originated in the American West and first appeared in print in an Ellensburgh, Washington, newspaper in 1889, according to the Oxford English Dictionary.

New waves of hobos were added after the depression of 1894, World War I, the Great Depression, World War II, the Korean conflict, and the Vietnam War. With the economic malaise of the 1980s, another jump came. Mostly, hobos are found west of the Mississippi River, where the country is open and the distance between cities vast. Hoboing is possible in the East,

* *Works Progress Administration.*

but it is far more difficult because of the winters and simply because you cannot ride very far—the cities are so close to each other.

Even though Blackie seriously began riding the rails in the Great Depression, he left the road a number of times. This is not unusual, since few hobos live their entire lives exclusively on the rails; it is a life they go in and out of depending on the vagaries of money, marital troubles, and boredom. Blackie had pretty much been a full-time hobo since the early 1980s. Over the years, he'd had jobs and he'd quit jobs.

"I'd get some scratch in my pocket and I'd hear that fucking engine hollering, 'Blackie, c'mon!'" he said with a burst of enthusiasm. When the urge came, the job was a casualty.

"I'd say, 'can you use that pen over there?' Yeah. I'd say, 'write out my check and I'm gone.' Oh, you can't quit. 'Oh yeah?' Yeah. It's like my friends, who work forty years at the same fucking job, then they retire and six months later, they're dead. So he works forty years to pay for the fucking house. He's got a little old camper, maybe a fishing boat, what the fuck's he got? Hasn't been no further than the fucking county line all his life. You think everything is right, and all of a sudden it's fucking wrong. One guy up here in the rice mill, he's got twenty years in. Now they're going to close it down. What's he gonna do?

"They want to keep up with the Joneses. What are you showin'? Why the hell do I gotta compete with that guy over there? That's America. They are greedy, jealous people. Back in the twenties, before the Depression, they were just as greedy as they are now. Yeah, now they're still greedy. Everything's goin' up. Fucking wages ain't goin' up. The fucking president says we can't give these people more minimum wage. What are they gonna do? When we ain't at war, having battles, killing people, fucking people up, selling planes, tanks, munitions, and so forth, we ain't making no fucking money. Right now, we're in a fucking slump again."

I didn't yet know Blackie well enough to probe how much longer a nearly seventy-seven-year-old man could continue living the hobo life: yet I did ask if he ever thought he would again return to citizen life.

"Oh, hell no. Hell with 'em. Every time I get something, somebody else always wants it. I'm better off right here, Dale. Right here, a fucking bum. I'm happy. Hey, this is my life. Fuck them people man, I don't need no nine-to-five shit. If I want to drink all night, I do. If I wanna wake up ten o'clock in the morning, I do. Or I get up at five like I did this morning. Free. That's what I mean. That's all I want. You know what life is, doncha? The only reason you hang around is to see what happens next. If it wouldn't be for curiosity, you'da hung it up, committed suicide, jumped off the 'Frisco bridge. That's all life is, man. You never know what's gonna happen. Wake up in the morning, put your feet on the floor, you can say what a shitty day it's gonna be. I say what a beautiful day."

Each of those early visits, I carefully set a tape recorder on a table or chair near Blackie. I was coming, as mentioned, to record the old stories, but I must confess a second ulterior motive: I figured that I might be able to milk Blackie as fodder for an ill-fated novel on the homeless I was then working on. These selfish reasons kept me coming, but by the end of the first month, something had changed and neither reason seemed important. I don't remember exactly when this happened. All I know is I stopped bringing the recorder. I missed some good stories. I remember one about a rescue mission that required everyone to sit through religious services, known as "earbanging." The preacher was especially boring and the men restless and hungry. (In these kinds of missions, you first are earbanged, then fed.) One guy loudly farted, and then another, and pretty soon the entire congregation erupted in a cacophony of farts as the men tried to outdo each other. There was a bodacious smell, by Blackie's account. The reverend ignored the intestinal riot and outlasted the men's gas supply, preaching another hour.

"That guy could wear out a brass monkey," Blackie said.

I'd spent a lot of time over the years with homeless people, but always briefly, always for a story or a book. This was the first time I was drawn to spend time with homeless men for friendship. While my association with Blackie has obviously become a book, at that time I had no such intentions, nor did Michael. We had no idea where things were going. We were certain the world did not need another nonfiction homeless book. Our *Journey to Nowhere* was the first in the long line of these contemporary volumes, and each, especially *Journey,* has fallen short for one reason or another—reasons I will later delve into. We did not want to write about the camp for our newspaper, for to draw attention to the men would harm them in two ways: It would point them out to authorities, who would then be compelled to enforce all sorts of laws. It would also subject them to the notions of modern sound-bite newspaper journalism, a most abusive form of shorthand, serving no one, especially the readers, except to fill space between the advertisements. An editor would demand twenty inches of copy (if I was lucky), which is about 1,000 words, the length of the preface to this book; another editor would demand two, perhaps three photographs (in color!) from Michael. If we waited for Thanksgiving or Christmas, we might get twenty-five inches and four photos, because we'd be giving the readers their "holiday weeper," to remind them how good they have it.

It wasn't worth it.

Michael was busy and did not come around much those first weeks. One afternoon, I insisted we visit the camp. We played hooky from our jobs, drove across the river, and walked down the sandy path. Blackie was in his house. When I knocked, he nearly leaped out of the door.

"Wanna see my dick?" he asked.

Michael stammered and before we could speak, Blackie pulled out a foot-long rubber dildo.

"Found it in a dumpster," he said. Blackie earned a living by scavenging the trash behind the hotels on the avenue for $20 and $30 skin magazines—he would then sell them back to the shop owners, who would restock them.

"Guys buy them to jack off once and then throw them out. I get a half buck each for them," he said.

A few weeks later, we brought a woman friend along for a visit. Blackie came out of his shack and announced, "Dale, Mike, someone's stole my dick." Our friend was a bit horrified until he explained: someone had entered his house and taken the foot-long piece of rubber.

When I first met Blackie, I mentioned I wanted to ride a train with him. We talked about going to the hobo convention, held annually in Britt, Iowa. Michael already wanted to make pictures of Blackie on a train. I asked Blackie if he was interested in taking both of us to the convention.

"Goddamn right we're gonna ride," Blackie said. "Ride up into Spokane, go into Sandpoint. Sandpoint, then we'll take the high line and go up to Whitefish, Chester, Glendive, Williston, into Minot. Minot, shoot that fucker over the hill again into Fargo. Fargo, shoot across into Minnie. From there, backtrack into Sioux City, where my fucking house is."

Michael quickly grew to like Blackie and some of the other men. It was a good time on the shore. We came around often and learned more about the camp's dynamics. Herbert and Bill remained mysteries. Occasionally, a fellow named Luke would come tearing over the levee top, down into camp, running like a man being chased by a bear. Blackie would talk with Luke before he sped off. In spite of the oddness of the situation, Blackie was trying to help Luke become a hobo.

"I share with guys. If I got it, I'll share it. That's the hobo's way of life. Guy comes up and hollers 'hey camp,' I'll look him over, and if he looks okay, I'll say, 'yeah, c'mon in.' All the time I'm sittin' on my .38."

Greenhorns and real hobos were okay. Imposter hobos and wannabes bothered Blackie. He separated the real hobos from the fakes by asking questions.

"You might ask the railroad dick's name, any stupid thing, what happened in Illinois, where trains switch, the way to bumfuck Egypt, and if he don't know the answer to it, he never been there, and so you don't get accommodated."

Blackie had a host of gripes that loomed far larger than fake hobos. He'd been running into trouble like he'd never before seen, trouble that had been growing with each of the last ten years. His world had changed—it was harder to be a hobo. It didn't take long to find out that Blackie had come to this shore an angry man.

Traditional work was more difficult: he could never make a bet like he did in 1936 over who could find the largest "lump."

"I used to carry my rake, a broom, and a shovel," Blackie said of his long-standing habit of doing yard work. He added he doesn't look for that work anymore because of the trouble.

"Last time I got nailed was by McDonalds up here. I knocked on a couple doors, I was going to rake a couple leaves," Blackie said. A few people declined, then he knocked on one woman's door.

"She said yeah, you sit down right here. Shit, two cruiser cars pulled in for my fuckin' ass. Right before Christmas. I didn't bum her. I didn't panhandle, but the son'bitch come right on me."

This never happened in the Great Depression.

"Back then, the only time the cops would bug you is when you were uptown panhandling or messing with the citizens; other than that, not much."

Despite work being hard to get, Blackie rarely panhandled—like most hobos, Blackie preferred work.

"I just tell them I'm dirty, broke, and in dire need of a drink," he said of the few times he begged. "I don't say I'm hungry. Bad mistake."

He tried holding a sign that said "Will Work for Food." He'd stand in front of shopping centers and lay on the puppy look. But too many people were on to that one to just hand over money like he wanted. There was always some doubting citizen who'd ask if he was hungry, usually swells in business suits. He'd pour it on thick, but they wouldn't just give him a few bucks. Instead they gave him food. One man once bought him ham and eggs and watched him eat it. Blackie had to chow it down, even though he'd just had a big breakfast, to prove the citizen wrong. He'd suffered too many stomach aches to put up with any more of that kind of inconvenience.

Blackie blamed his troubles on the huge increase in people living on the streets. Blackie hated the word *homeless*. He didn't feel it applied to him. To call him homeless was an ultimate insult.

He was a hobo, not a homeless man, he would tell you emphatically.

"I don't like these so-called homeless," Blackie said. He went on a tirade. Blackie felt he was getting caught up in a problem that he had no part in.

"Two-bit so-called fucking homeless. You ever talked to these fucking homeless? You know how to catch them, doncha? 'I'm homeless, I'm this and I'm that'—the next thing that comes out of his mouth you say, 'hey, when's the last time you hear from your mother?' They tell ya' last week or somethin', an' I tell them you ain't homeless, you mother fucker. You got a mother. You got somewhere to go."

He was especially bothered by a family living in the camp south of Woody and Shorty's. We watched as two of the little girls in pretty dresses played on the levee bank.

"Shit, they got their welfare checks, and they're drinking them up. And who's hurtin'? The kids. I wish they'd change that. I wish they'd get them fuckin' kids outta here. Son of a bitch. The money is there. Somebody fucks up one of them girls, whose gonna get the rap? Us. Who we botherin'? Nobody. We drink a little wine, a little beer, enjoy ourselves, but you always got fuckers who are gonna come up here and ruin it. If they want to bug somebody, get the panhandlers out there, get the dopers. Get the families and kids the hell out of here, that's the main objective. Other than that, hell, this is great down here. We like it. I don't bother nobody, don't harm nobody, I want my peace and privacy and leave me the fuck alone. I ain't got an enemy in the world. If I have, I wish he'd come talk to me. That's the way I look at it."

While he was angry that the homeless were making it hard for hobos, Blackie knew some of the people he called homeless were having a hard go of it, just like in the Depression.

"You know that hotel up there?" he said, referring to a hotel that catered to single women with children on welfare. "She pays the $330 they want for rent, $150 deposit, you know what I mean. Fifty dollars cleaning fee. By the time she fries the first fucking egg, that is providing she went to Goodwill and bought a frying pan, cooking gear, and so forth, her $690 is gone. So what's she going to do the rest of the month? Eat shit?"

Blackie's ire was mostly reserved for the druggies and rough people among the homeless, a breed he seldom ran into in the old days. When he first moved to the west bank with a woman he was then living with, they camped upriver with the drug users, not knowing any better.

"I paid no attention to nothing. Got up in the morning, she always woke up before me. I sit up and have a cigarette, Son'bitch, she let out a scream. She was scared of bugs, rats, snakes. I thought ah, what's wrong with the bitch now? She come around, shakin' like a mother fucker. She'd wake up the fuckin' dead. I step out, here's this fucker swinging, number nine wire around his neck, tied up there, had a stool smaller than that table there. That's what they had him standing on. See, what happened, they had given him the bucks to go over to the store and he didn't come back. They decided to hang him, cut off his dick and balls and shoved them in his mouth."

A week later, an old man was incinerated in his sleeping bag, and a few days after that, a woman was raped.

"I said fuck you guys, I'm coming down here. In the old days, you had your dopers, you had everything, but they stuck in their own area . . . the hobos stayed over that way, and the winos stayed downtown."

Now the druggies and prostitutes were moving downriver, toward his camp. He couldn't escape them.

As December neared, Woody and Shorty started moving into the camp's circle and we got to know them. Road Dog, an old friend of Blackie's, came off the rails with Helga to winter over in the camp. By sheer volume, the hobos of Blackie's Camp claimed an important strip of the shore, and this kept at bay the worst of the troublemakers.

In spite of all these people, each time I came, Blackie usually was sitting alone at the round table or fire ring, looking off at the river. Or he would be walking the levee top, by the siding tracks, in deep thought. It seemed he looked forward to our visits as much as we did. Michael was coming more often, and I felt a bit jealous that he was getting closer to Blackie and the boys, as we came to call the men of the camp. I would occasionally see a woman with dark hair walking her two dogs, Great Danes. She had the look of a Kansas farm woman; she usually wore blue jeans and a pullover sweater. Sometimes she talked with Blackie. Sometimes this mysterious woman just watched from a distance. When she saw us, she often got in her car and drove off.

No HOBO IS AN ISLAND: the world of the hobo jungle is a community of friends and neighbors. Between them are alliances, disputes, jealousies, misinterpretations, secrets, the need for love, the need to be noticed and applauded, the fear of alienation.* Blackie was surrounded by a revolving cast of some forty River People who called the west bank home. While you could not call Blackie king of the hobo jungle (such a term is pure Hollywood, used by wannabe weekend hobos who have fine day jobs), Blackie was a mayor of sorts of this community. If he was not sought out for advice, he was at least respected as an elder statesman of the road world.

Here, in no particular order of importance, are twelve main characters, human and animal, surrounding Blackie. All were critical to Blackie for companionship or for the acquisition of life's necessities.

WOODY AND SHORTY

You could not say one of the names of these two men without the other, for it would not come naturally off the tongue. They were inseparable. If Shorty was alone, you could count on Woody being nearby, suddenly popping from behind a tree or coming out of a tent, or you would at least hear his voice in the distance. "We're partners, we watch out for each other," they would say, often in unison. They lived in a tent the next camp down from Blackie, and though they seemed obscure characters at first, their importance would grow. Both were bearded, rough-looking men (you would feel fearful meeting them on a deserted street if you did not know better), and both were much kinder than their appearance.

Shorty, well, was short. He was quite conscious of his height and if you knew him, you could make endless commentary about his stature, but if you did not know him, he would gladly beat you up. He was absolutely fearless. Shorty took on all numbers and sizes of men; in the time I knew him, he suffered many scrapes and bruises and once even a crushed windpipe that prevented him from talking for many days. He'd even fought cops when they'd had him cuffed by butting them with his head like a goat. I think Shorty won as many fights as he lost. Shorty was born in New Jersey. He spent time in prison back East some two decades earlier, after he

---

In other words, they're just like us.

shot the kneecap off of a friend who had assaulted a woman who was traveling with them in a car. Shorty's situation was made worse because he stabbed the man in the back three times while they were in jail. He'd spent twenty of his fifty years as a hobo, and he had four grown children. He sometimes would travel back East to meet his adult sons. Michael grew fond of Shorty, perhaps because both men shared similar backgrounds up to their preteen years; both were orphaned and impoverished, but instead of coming out of the experience a citizen, Shorty became a hobo. Like Blackie, he tried the regular world and gave up on it.

"You know the difference between you and me?" Shorty once asked us. "You told your boss to go to hell and started to walk out, but he held up your check and said you'll be back for this. You went back. I didn't."

Woody was more of an enigma. He had some mental affliction for which he needed medicine. While Shorty did not like crowds or being inside walls, strictly as a matter of taste, a group of strangers or a confined area was something of a terror for Woody. He was made nervous by anything out of the ordinary, and he sometimes stuttered. Woody once talked about someone he was mad at, and he told us, "I'll squeeze him and put him asleep, like I done in Wyoming." He faced some manslaughter charge that he got out of, but we never heard the details.

The men had become partners the previous year. They met right after Woody had broken both legs jumping off a fast-moving train. Shorty helped him recover, and they became friends while drinking at a favorite hobo bar across the river that was next to the Union Pacific mainline. Before coming to this side of the river, they'd lived in an abandoned metal building near our newspaper. When that building was torn down, they set up a tent just south of Blackie's house.

LUKE

Luke is a classic example of what Maxim Gorky called a Creature That Once Was a Man. On our first meeting while sitting at Blackie's fire, I felt him beyond approach, too weird for understanding. I remember him running as fast as a person could down the bank, with his shirt off in the cold weather, heaving and sweating. He wore earphones plugged into a pocket stereo, and we could hear the music blaring. He was well over six feet tall and muscular. He blathered and drooled and we did not understand much—it sounded something like *Dowee ahha blippin ya ya. Ya!* Then he ran off, came back, said something similar, then raced to points unknown. He was one of those people you see talking to themselves who might prompt you to cross a public street, and I never spent the time it takes to get to know such a person.

After many months, we became good friends. He stopped being incoherent, talking in a formal voice. "Why Dale, it is nice to see you," he would say when we met. He grew rather normal. I was never certain if his initial oddness was a defense mechanism. I once was interviewing a woman who ran a shelter in Los Angeles's Skid Row, when she glanced out her window and said, "Oh, Joe's masturbating again," referring to a large man lying in a parking lot across the street. After sending a worker to talk with the man, she explained he masturbated to scare people away; many street people have different "crazy" responses to ward off trouble.

Luke was born in the state of Washington. His mother died when he was young. He did not like the way things were going with his father and ran away from home at age sixteen. When we met him, he was thirty-five and had never been off of the road. He never had received any help and was now for the first time trying to get Supplemental Security Income (SSI), the federal disability monies given to handicapped people, but he had not yet been approved. He had two dreams. One was to buy a truck so he could collect aluminum cans at distant points beyond where men with shopping carts could go. The second dream, far more important, was to become a hobo. This is why he came around the camp, to learn from the masters.

Luke wanted to become the best hobo in all the West. He was excited about proving himself.

ALICE AND BURT

This couple, with almost no teeth between them (Burt has tatoos enough for six people), had the look of classic Joadian Okies who came to California but never made it. They lived in a van and later a trailer atop the levee just north of Blackie's Camp. They had a lot of grit, especially Alice. She'd been active on the Sacramento side of the river in fighting for homeless rights. Burt was an oil roughneck who had not had regular work in many months.

They had a son of maybe sixteen who we never saw go to school and a pitbull by the name of Jaws. Jaws begged Burt to lower a tree branch near their camp. The dog would bite on it and Burt would let it go, allowing the dog to spring ten feet off the ground. It would hang this way for as long as forty-five minutes, until it was bleeding at the gums. Burt would bring the dog down, but it would soon beg to be put back in the tree.

Their van was perpetually broken. When I saw them in early August, before I came to know Blackie, they were putting in a radiator. Burt had been trying to solder it over a campfire to fix a leak, with little success. It took them a month to get the radiator in. A few months later, the van was again stranded on the shore, in need of a starter.

ROAD DOG AND HELGA

Road Dog is a famous West Coast hobo, if for nothing other than his cartoonlike logo we'd seen scrawled on dozens of boxcars over the years. He was a long-time partner of No Thumbs, murdered three weeks after we last saw him in 1982, going past our train that was sided for a northbound out of the Roseville yard.

I wasn't surprised when Road Dog showed up in camp with Helga (his latest girlfriend, who was overweight out of proportion to the thinness of Road Dog and was also pregnant), because Road Dog knows all the old hobos. Road Dog came to winter over until the spring riding weather and to hide from the cops, for he said he was wanted for prison escape.

Road Dog was a tall and quiet man with a rising forehead and a slight gray beard, though I don't think he was much past forty-five or so. He had the hard-angled head common to poor white folks. He became a hobo as a teenager after he ran away from home and went down to the tracks. The old hobos told him to go back to his parents. He said that if they sent him away, he'd jump on a car behind them. They let him into the circle, and he'd been a hobo since. His eyes lit up when I mentioned No Thumbs, and he spoke in reverent terms, then became very sad.

There was something dark about Road Dog. He told a story about the time he and Shotgun Joe were sharing a boxcar with two strangers as they went up the Feather River Canyon, a long ride through fifty-some tunnels in California's Cascade Mountains. At night when the train topped out of the canyon, the two strangers pulled a gun. They ordered Road Dog and Shotgun Joe to strip and then jump out of the train then going sixty miles an hour. The two men were snickering. Road Dog took off his shirt and was stalling for time. He was by the door. Joe was still sitting. Road Dog was working real slow. The guys with the gun told him to hurry, and he went for his zipper. Just then, Joe pulled out a sawed-off double barrel shotgun with both hammers cocked and said "okay, mother fuckers." The two strangers told Road Dog and Joe they were just joking. "Fuck you," Road Dog said, "you wun't. Now you're gonna strip. And gonna jump out." They made them strip and jump. When the train got in to Portola, they made themselves scarce. They never knew if the two men survived.

VERA

Vera, a stout and short woman with a pleasant personality, was a citizen who lived in a house and was always around the camp. She told us she was saved from this river by the man she met who took her into his home. She had cancer and told us she didn't expect to live, but she survived. She hung around the men and was friends with all of them, though she hated Alice, and Alice hated her. Vera cooked the men a Thanksgiving turkey, made them Christmas dinner. Vera was typical of the several citizens who came to visit the camp (with the exception of us), in that she at one time had been homeless.

MARTIN

Martin was a steelworker at a Lorain, Ohio, mill until it shut down. He had followed a long and difficult road seeking real work. When we met him, he had just landed a job at a nearby small manufacturing plant and was sending money to his family still back in the middle part of the country. No one at the plant knew he was homeless. He lived out of his truck at a place other than the river. He came often, bringing Blackie firewood and helping the guys out in other ways.

TIE-TIE, MOOSE, AND MISTER

Tie-Tie was born on the west bank of the river, the offspring of a dog belonging to other River People. Blackie took it in, in spite of his already having Moose, a big friendly mongrel.

"Hey, let the fleas alone and come over here. Get your ass over here," he would say affectionately to Tie-Tie. "Got a kiss for Daddy?" The dog would kiss him. Moose was named after a dog Blackie had years before, a St. Bernard with a pleasant disposition. Eventually the St. Bernard got so old it couldn't walk, and Blackie knew it was dying. He sat there for four hours with a gun, drinking away, but he couldn't bring himself to shoot the dog. Finally, a friend came. They took it to a veterinarian. The veterinarian told him it would cost ten bucks to put the dog away. "I told him I didn't care if it cost a hundred," Blackie said. The new Moose was equally revered.

Mister was a once feral black cat that was too friendly for its own good. The cat made its living off the largess of men who had little to spare. Mister, claimed by no one, successfully claimed everyone.

THE FIRE BURNED TALL IN THE METAL RING. Michael was taking a picture of Blackie down at Woody and Shorty's camp. I was seated in my usual chair, looking out at the river before it was lost to the night. My world was across the water: an office and a home that was just five blocks from that office. That was the "real world." There was a boss, deadlines, a mortgage, fees for utilities, a car to maintain, critical career decisions, and so on. In front of me was Blackie's house, his world. I could hear Blackie telling a story downriver and the laughter of others. Blackie did not have a boss, deadlines, a mortgage or any of the other bills, or critical career decisions.

We'd been regularly visiting for well over a month. In that time, Blackie and the boys *never* asked about our world. This was something that would continue, and it puzzled us. It did not matter how much money we made, whether or not we owned homes, or what kind of social lives we led. We could have been millionaires, but in the camp, we were just two guys, Dale and Michael, like the others who hung out on the shore. Perhaps there was no reason for them to inquire about us. They knew our world. They'd once been there. They made a choice to leave it, or at least they told us they made the choice.

Our world, for those of us who call ourselves "middle class"—and I assume the majority of you who can afford to buy this book fall into at least the lower spectrum of this group— is made up of basic rules and assumptions that forbid most of us from understanding or even accepting other realities. There are prescribed ways to live, be it working, what we purchase, how we spend our leisure time, who we associate with, what we perceive to be the "in" thing to do. We are a much more Germanic society than we care to admit. Michael once photographed a lookalike contest at a shopping mall for the popular singer Madonna. When confronted with a dozen girls who were all made up exactly like the flamboyant pop idol, he asked why they came. "To express our individuality," one said.

Blackie did not go to shopping malls. But he intersected with this class of people in the form of boaters passing by on the river. Most warm days, they throttled in front of the camp. Some of the boaters were quite wealthy by appearance, in cabin cruisers or sleek cigarette boats, or were aboard a fake paddlewheel tourist boat with people drinking and dancing to the tune of Big Band music as the vessel went by each dusk. There was a grand view of the river from camp, and thus

REALITY
VERSUS
REALITY

the boaters had a grand view of Blackie. The boaters, I imagine, did not see Blackie as an elder hobo with a life of stories they would pay to hear in a more civilized setting. I'm sure they saw a wastrel. I know this because when I sat there alone and studied these boaters, I saw their looks.

Some acted as though they weren't looking, but they always stared sideways. A few waved. Neither kind ever stopped to talk. There was an invisible barrier far more impenetrable than the one-time wall that separated Berlin. The boaters, even the ones who waved, could not pull ashore to talk because they were uninterested (even though they stared), were afraid, or had preconceived notions.

Many of us are figurative boaters when we see someone without a home. Readers come to a story about the homeless or hobos in the newspapers, on television, or in this book and judge them (from a comfortable distance) through the prism of their own reality, usually middle class in origin.

I've seen this numerous times after I have written articles or responded to callers when I've appeared on radio talk shows. The people on the other end of the line usually express attitudes that go something like this: "If I can work and support myself in this society, why can't *those* people? *They* must have done something wrong or must be lazy or dumb. *They* deserve what has happened."

This attitude often allows readers to not only justify inaction (like boaters, to gun the engine and race on, content with their own enjoyment), but to confirm their own version of reality.

Such labeling obscures deeper issues. There are uncountable numbers of homeless. Behind them are millions of poor, many working in low-paying jobs, who are ill housed, scarcely hanging on. Behind them, further removed from the edge but pushing toward it, are still more, like so many soldiers in one of those old European wars marching in columns to become fodder for the cannons. The numbers are numbing. It's all too much to think about in any terms but as boaters. The poor are failures in a society that worships winners. (The only thing we relish more than winners are winners who fall from grace and self-destruct before our eyes.)

Many people in the political center are suspect of stories about the poor, as are those on the right and (especially) liberals on the left, for radically different reasons. A writer comes to this subject like a salesperson condemned to peddle gasoline in hell. The method of approach is suspect by all sides in all efforts to write about poverty. The mere act is political, no matter how innocent the writer's motives.

One would think that to write a book on a subject as monolithic as the homeless (or their hobo brothers) in our faltering but still wealthy nation would be an easy job. It is, after all, a dramatic story. Yet the ways to err are many. You cannot make real people "art." You cannot truly take a journey into their inner psyche. You walk a line between being maudlin and cruel. Superficiality is a lurking danger. If I were to curse a thinking man or woman, I would wish on them the task of writing a "homeless book."

A writer must consider general attitudes toward someone like Blackie. Because this book is not a work of fiction, but is more or less a journalistic exercise—a form that has its damnable rules, with simplification as its essence—it is at this point that I'm supposed to explain Blackie in context with middle-class reality.

I face serious choices in packaging Blackie.

{ SOLUTION 1 } — I could romanticize Blackie, make him a noble gentleman of the road, a mythical elfin man who dances and sings and tells funny stories. This would appeal to the nostalgists and would keep others from thinking him a misfit.

{ PROBLEM } — I've written enough about this subject to know that all you good liberals fear this most of all, that we might try to sell you on the fact that these are happy-go-lucky wanderers, like they come off in those silly Hollywood movies. Or worse, we could be trying to convince you that they are content with their poverty, like some latter-day slaves singing in the fields.

{ SOLUTION 2 } — I could go even further and canonize his life by not telling the whole truth, hiding all the warts. I could present the flawless Blackie, the ultimate victim. To take this approach to the extreme, I could altogether stop writing about Blackie and instead choose to focus on the Murrays, his neighbors who arrived on the shore in February, a family of a man and woman and three young boys. I could make you weep with their story, with little effort, ensuring perhaps greater sales and thus profits for this enterprise.

{ PROBLEM } — Using the family would be too easy. Other writers have pandered to women and children, who deserve our compassion, of course, but as the writer Peter Marin has noted, 80 percent of the homeless are men who hurt and cry the same as all humans, all macho posturing aside. Do men deserve any less sympathy? Besides being dishonest, this approach ensures that all you conservatives with feet rooted deep in the verdant moss that grows rich on the fertilizer of these times would say we are presenting the homeless as pitiable saints who should be showered with our precious tax dollars in an effort to ensure their salvation.

{ SOLUTION 3 } — I could explain in weighty detail the cruel changes to our economy, the human weakness, and the bad luck that lead someone to sink into the abyss. I could write about falling wages, the cost of housing, failing schools, and so on—all perfectly sensible things to discuss.

{ PROBLEM } — This usually becomes a mumbling morass of stupidity. Those among you who know these things would glaze over because you've heard them a thousand times. Those of you in the top 20 percent of wealth who believe anyone can and should become a millionaire (just work hard and vote Republican) have never listened to these things anyway and simply don't believe them. Even the working-class skeptics among you would hold Blackie's life to your standards, ultimately dismissing him like so many turds being flushed down a toilet.

No. I've publicly made some of these mistakes in dozens of newspaper articles and at least one book. I discard them all. If we are blessed, all political camps, left and right, will curse us, but I will not do violence to Blackie by trying to explain him in the context of middle-class reality. There is a hobo reality, and trying to define it is like trying to tell you about a planet in which hydrogen instead of oxygen is the element that fuels life and in which gravity is half that of earth. Briefly, however, I will say that in relation to middle-class reality, Blackie makes no excuses for himself. Blackie said he made a choice and does not ask any quarter except to be left alone. He does not consider himself homeless.

He does *not* want your sympathy.

Of course, I can point to hundreds of homeless people I have interviewed over the years who are desperate for a job and a home, who suffer mental or physical afflictions beyond their control. I can tell you about shuttered steel mills and middle-aged workers destroyed by the closings, too old for new jobs, too young for retirement. I can show you starving children by the score. (These are victims, and you must understand that I differentiate between them and hobos such as Blackie.) If you are a Calvinist, social Darwinist, Reaganite, or some such thing, you may be inclined to argue against them, blaming them for their collective misery. But you will not be able to use those arguments against Blackie. Blackie was emphatic that he was different—he made a choice to give up a regular job and home and said he was quite happy with it. His life seemed to boil down to this: a long time ago, a man tried the system (middle-class reality) and did not like it. He rode the rails and went back to again try the system. Again, he did not like it. He went back and forth several times, until—well into old age—he switched to living an alternate life to which he was drawn. He was out of the closet; he was a hobo, not a citizen.

Yet I have long grappled with this issue of "choice." I have wondered if someone could voluntarily make a decision to forgo a civilized existence for a hard life on the road. In the times I have heard this word *choice* from various hobos, I wondered if it was a hollow excuse for a decision that had been forced on them—you know, in the way people would put the best face on a bad situation, like a man who has had both legs cut off in an accident say it was a good thing, because he was tired of walking anyway. I hoped in getting to know Blackie, I would find out if he was telling the truth about his choice. If he wasn't lying to me, was he lying to himself?

On the surface, one aspect of choice for a hobo is the difference between the concrete versus the abstract. I believe it is actually easier to deal with a lion bursting through the front door— you can fight it off by beating it with a chair. A lion is a definite enemy, a certain nightmare. It is far worse to deal with the thousand rats running up out of the dark cellar, chewing at you from all directions, for no matter how you try to crush them, they'll eventually get you.

Our reality is abstract, full of an ever-marching horde of rats. Blackie's reality is concrete: two lions, the procurement of food and shelter.

We work to earn our food and shelter, but laboring in an office, retail store, or factory is a relatively modern concept. Before there was such a thing as money, humans built huts and foraged for their own food and bartered for other goods. There was no such thing as "unemployment." Now that the economies of the modern world are based on dollars, we must work to get dollars to trade for our needs. With this comes many troubles. Blackie took Jefferson's agrarian ideal and pushed it back one step further—he merely cut out this middle work, returning somewhat to a subsistence level. He digs through trash bins for food or fishes it from the river and lives in a hut he built himself for nearly free. (The need for friendship exists, of course, but that comes naturally and does not have to be sought.)

If Blackie made a choice to turn to this kind of existence, he of course left behind another life, one with women and children and jobs. We'd learned a lot about Blackie's hobo life. He kept his other life mostly hidden. He was very careful about this. In retrospect, he was either brilliant at masking it, or he had erased it from memory. I cannot say which is the case.

From what we could gather from what little he told us, he had four or six girls, from two marriages; a third marriage produced no children. As I look over recorded transcripts, there is much confusion and contradiction over where he had his children and with which women he had them. He wasn't sure where his daughters were, though he thought one was in Florida, another in Maine, another in Utah. At one point, he said he lived back east for twelve years, which would explain the Boston accent. He said he lived in Santa Barbara; Provo, Utah; and Sioux City, Iowa.

"Far as my wife goes, she's dead," he told us. "She died of cancer on me, the one I had the four daughters by. Second old lady, that son'bitch, over in Provo, Utah. And that place in Iowa, I'm going to let the redhead have it."

Whatever the situation—whoever his people were—I believe Blackie was speaking very honestly when he looked at me and said, "Dale, I disgraced them all."

He said he was in World War II, in northern Africa and Germany, then again in Korea, when a plane he was in was shot down. The war was only talked about one afternoon, when we asked. He said he got disability benefits from Korea. He told us he didn't get social security, but did not explain why not.

Blackie worked contracting, electrical engineering, auto salvage. He freely told us he spent time in jail on charges ranging from petty theft to larceny. The biggest case was a counterfeiting charge in the early 1950s, when he said he was printing $20 notes, using his name as the treasurer of the United States on the bills. In the 1970s, Blackie says his sister committed him. He was in for over a month. He was drinking, he said, but wasn't crazy. He said she put him away to get the family money.

I wanted to know all I could about Blackie. Several years after that winter we spent at Blackie's Camp, I started to check the paper trail to see how true his stories were. I went to the Santa Barbara courthouse where he said he had been found guilty of various crimes, and sure enough, every case he told us about was on file.

The most recent case was in 1986, when Blackie was convicted of taking four used radiators from an auto parts store at which he once worked—he was last seen leaving with them stacked in his shopping cart as a getaway car of sorts. In that period, he was picked up several times for drinking in public and firing a gun. In 1958, court records show he was sent to state prison for a burglary committed in Santa Barbara; in 1967, he was convicted of larceny in Klamath Falls, Oregon; he was also convicted of petty theft in 1978. I tried to look into the matter of the commitment, but such files are forbidden to the public due to privacy laws. He gave me the name of the sister and the city in which she lived, but there was no telephone listing for her.

Blackie had showed us paperwork with his name on it for the Sioux City house where his most recent wife lived. He said he visited her two years earlier. I called information and there was no listing. I then checked with a librarian, who used the cross directory to give me phone numbers for neighbors on either side of the address. A woman who'd lived there fifteen years said she didn't know Blackie and told me the house had been torn down five years earlier.

The military will not release the records of veterans without their permission. I never asked Blackie to write such permission, so I cannot confirm any of his military service.

I was set to dig deeper, but something stopped me.

Of course, I wondered about the veracity of his stories, and this was a good reason to continue probing. Woody at one point said you can't believe everything Blackie says. Michael said that probably parts of his stories were true and parts of them were stretched, as with any true hobo. I mean, how could we believe the story about the man who picked him up in the hobo jungle and brought him home to make love to his wife, after he showed his penis—a tube he carried in his pocket to enable him to urinate, because his organ was shot off in the war? But it was so bizarre it might have happened. He did not hide his brushes with the law, and maybe these other less damning things occurred.

I guess I stopped digging because I realized none of this mattered one bit. Blackie could be boldly lying about his jobs and family—and so what? I did not need to talk with his children, his former bosses, his wives. It was not just that I was delving into the life of someone who had become a friend, a life he obviously did not want to parade before the world. He materialized on the shore of the river, as if riding the rods beneath the boxcar of a steam train puffing out of the mist of the Great Depression, a hobo out of time and place coming into our world, our reality, and his existence before us was all we needed to see. Often, I am sorry when I meet famous people, for their image is more compelling than the disappointing reality of the face-to-face encounter. Sometimes, you are better off not meeting the famous person. In the same way, I did not want to meet the Blackie of the reality we all know.

YOU CAN FEEL TROUBLE COMING ON THE STREET. It has an odor, and it comes when things have been going too well. Blackie had not seen trouble in months. He was off the bottle (save for a social beer now and then), had a great camp, good friends. Yet Blackie smelled trouble. He warned us it was coming before any of it happened.

The first of the trouble came in early December with the death of Tie-Tie. Blackie was coming back from a food run when the dog ran out into traffic. Blackie watched Tie-Tie slowly bleed to death. When I showed up at camp one day, he pointed to the grave between his and Herbert's houses, marked with a multitude of flowers.

Things were progressing with the hotel and condo project upriver. The new city was about to raze the nearby old men's whitewashed shacks that rented for something less than a hundred bucks a month. The talk was the city was trying to get rid of poor people to change its image to attract more such development.

"Broderick is Broderick," Vera said with contempt. "No matter how they try to change it, it's still going to be Broderick."

And more people were streaming to the west bank because the police were busy across the river pushing them out of camps. There were more families with children, as well as more druggies.

A big sweep was coming, according to rumor, to drive the River People away from the Broderick shore. The only other sweep in modern memory along the west bank happened several years earlier, when there was a national speedboat race. The town's administrators didn't want visitors to view any River People. That time, they drove them off and burned their camps with flamethrowers. This new trouble seemed more ominous.

We heard the sweep would happen before Christmas. We told Blackie and the boys to run to a pay phone and call us the moment the sweep went down.

For many days, the camp was glum. We'd come and just sit, not talk about much. Blackie wasn't telling his stories. One night, we found him and the others just staring at the fire. Shorty said he had a fishing license and that meant you could camp, because people had a right to camp when they were fishing. Woody said he had a U.S. Forest Service campfire permit and that made it legal. He produced the permit, which he said entitled him to build a fire. In order to build a fire, you had to camp so you could tend it.

THE STAND

"You know what this is?" Blackie asked. "Flood control district, brother. Above that dike, yeah, they can mess with us. From that dike down is nothing but flood control, operated by the corps of engineers, that's Uncle Sam. They have no jurisdiction."

The men sought all points of argument that would build a case in favor of their staying. Blackie didn't know where he could go if the sweep came down. He worried that no matter where he went, the cops would mess with him. He was too old to bedroll under the stars, or more likely in this winter season, the rain, as he might have done in younger days. He told us he just wanted to remain until he could hop a train for the now-cold north country, where hobos were still tolerated. But he said this without conviction.

It was cold. The men heaped wood on the fire and held council into the night. Bill and Herbert were in no mood to fight anyone and were hanging somewhere beyond the light of the fire and the gas lantern suspended from a rafter of Blackie's porch. Woody and Shorty drank and the more Shorty did, the more he wanted to fight. Shorty was ready to take on the whole of the world. Blackie didn't need booze to make him listen.

"We'll go to court and demand a jury trial," Shorty suggested. "That's it, we'll demand a jury trial."

The words *jury trial* were repeated dozens of times, like a war cry, and they worked themselves up to find joy in the fact that they were going to court if the cops did come. If they got a jury trial before the citizens of Broderick, they felt they could win. What began as a somber evening ended with the men stoked with excitement. Shorty was the most enthusiastic. Shorty liked a good fight—he would have fought a gang of Hell's Angels if they came at him. Blackie was enthusiastic for different reasons: I think he saw no other option. Woody was the most afraid of the three, but if Shorty was going to fight with him, Woody could stand being around strangers. "I stick with Shorty," Woody said.

They asked what we thought. We feared coaching them in any way, for we were still working daily journalists. The last thing you want when you are a working journalist is to be accused of encouraging or orchestrating situations, or even merely having an opinion. Then you can be charged with bias, which runs contrary to the cold sugarless oatmeal that most newspapers feed their readers these days.

Yet I had some ideas.

"You can play this for a good run. You can make the city of West Sacramento look like it is run by blathering sons of Nazis. We'll make this camp even more spiffy. We'll put aluminum siding on the houses, bring in some sod, plant marigolds. We'll put up a pole topped with the biggest American flag money can buy so they can see it all the way over at the Capitol Building. We'll call it Liberty Camp. You'll bake apple pies in that oven and feed the journalists who will come by the dozens and give you national media attention. You are doing something real in a world that is fake. You are making a stand. You can say *fuck you!* to the whole country."

I wanted to say this. But I did not.

"Sounds like a good idea," I said instead. I added just one observation: while they awaited the court date for their jury trial, they would not yet have been found guilty of illegal camping; thus the police could not evict them. Even if they eventually lost, they would beat the city for a while. The men saw beauty in this, holding the idea up for study as one might hold a fine bottle of bourbon to the light before it is drunk. They marveled at the concept of benefiting from the American legal system. These were men who had never challenged authority but had spent their lives with authority challenging them.

I had scheduled a trip to visit the woman I'd lived with until she moved away to England. Just days after I left, on December 8, the cops moved in. Michael was there. The officers marched down the shore and wrote warnings, tacking up signs proclaiming the illegality of camping on the bank. The main cop was Sgt. Ronald Wilson. He made men roll up their sleeves to look for needle marks. His officers (who lacked warrants) then searched shopping carts and dug through the houses.

The warnings were written on slips of paper that said if anyone was still on the shore in one week, they would be arrested. On December 15, Sgt. Wilson called the media and led a pack of reporters and camerapeople along the bank, unlike the unannounced sweep of a week earlier. Michael told me that the sergeant was surprised to find Blackie and Woody and Shorty nervously sitting in the camp waiting to be arrested. The sergeant had made no plans to arrest anyone, for he figured none of the River People would stay put. River People were supposed to run. The sergeant wrote out citations that ordered the men to appear in court on January 16. The men were disappointed. They wanted to be arrested on the spot.

When I came back to the United States a few days later, the men recounted the sweep. Woody had been freaked out by the television cameras. "I need my medicine!" Michael recalled him crying. Woody said it was Michael who saved him. "I told them to get back! Michael told them and they moved!" Woody said of when Michael whispered to the other reporters not to interview Woody but to talk with Blackie or Shorty instead.

The cops suggested that Blackie go to a rescue mission. They were playing to the media, for the cops had to avoid appearing as if they were stomping on the homeless without an offer of help. The cops had learned from their Sacramento counterparts across the river how to conduct a proper publicity campaign. I don't know if Blackie tried to tell the television crews that he was not homeless but that he was a hobo, and hobos live where they belong, in hobo jungles, not missions. If he did, it must have sounded silly. The argument could not possibly fit into a soundbite even if he pulled it off with brilliance.

"Mission stiffs," Blackie said with contempt about going to a shelter. He would go, he said, "like a snowball in hell—about the same damn difference." He would sooner go back to city life. A mission was the equivalent of prison. "Missions started back in England and come over here. You get a bowl of fucking pea water called soup."

The next few weeks were uneventful except for the coming and going of Christmas, which was not really celebrated except for Vera cooking the men a meal. There was a building tension in the camp. The men rehearsed various scenarios. Vera and Alice encouraged them—Alice had fought the Sacramento cops several years earlier, partaking in a protest campout on the steps of the county administration building. She knew a thing or two about bucking the system.

If this story was fiction, especially a Hollywood movie, the cops would be the perfect villains, for a story such as this, if it were indeed a movie, would require simplicity. But in real life, the police are not the ultimate bad guys. I spent some time writing about homeless bashing for the newspaper and found fourteen California cities were then sweeping the homeless. In each case, I learned the police never initiated the sweeps. They were merely following orders to go after the homeless, orders that came from politicians acting on behalf of merchants (who respond to complaints from customers) or developers. I know officers who find no joy in routing the homeless (one once called the newspaper office and tipped us to a secret sweep in Sacramento), yet the cops unfairly take the brunt of all blame. Often the police are merely agents for the people who hold the real power, the ones who never dirty their hands.

In my research for that story, I discovered that modern homeless sweeps are far more vicious than during the Great Depression, at least in California. The reason is that in the 1930s, the homeless had an economic value. The monied interests needed them at key times of the year to pick crops such as fruit or cotton. Thus, there was more tolerance. Today, there is no economic value seen in the homeless, only economic loss. Plus, many citizens rightly fear some of the more violent homeless, the same ones Blackie dreaded. Collectively, the homeless do seem more violent than in days of old, perhaps because there are now more of the mentally ill on the streets. Blackie was correct when he said things are worse today.

It was a brittle time in camp as the men waited for the court date. Something was going on with Bill and Herbert, Blackie's silent campmates, and it seemed best to stay away for a while. In the quiet before the court case, a few River People who didn't want to fight had drifted back to sleep in the weeds, including Alice and Burt.

When the court day came, we went down to the camp early. Blackie and the boys were already gone. We went to the courthouse, located in a former supermarket. (The newly incorporated city of West Sacramento was very poor.) Harry had driven the men over in his bus, and they were inside drinking beers. They had done little to prepare. They wore their normal clothes, which is to say pants and shirts reclaimed from trash bins or bought for coins from thrift stores. If any attempt had been made to clean up, it was not evident.

The men were nervous, especially Woody. They left the bus and stood outside smoking some roll-your-owns. Realizing they had to do something to make themselves more presentable, they used the mirrors and window glass of parked cars to slick back the unwashed grayness of their hair. They talked about the justness of their cause.

"We aren't bothering no one," said Blackie. "They say we're a public nuisance. There isn't any public near us." He gloated when he pulled his citation, in which the cop had incorrectly written that he was three feet four inches tall and had placed last year's date at the top.

The judge was running late. Nine o'clock came and went, and the men were still outside smoking. Slowly, things got underway, and Blackie and the boys filtered in. Herbert and Vera had come to watch.

The courtroom was crowded with people sitting on chairs set in uneven rows in what appeared to have been the main produce section of the former market. The bailiff was about as streetworn by appearance as Shorty. He ordered everyone to find a seat. There were few chairs; Woody hesitated and the bailiff barked. Woody stammered. Shorty ran to defend his partner— he didn't like it when people picked on Woody. The bailiff turned to view who was yelling at him and saw Shorty wore a duck-billed baseball cap. "Take off that hat," the bailiff demanded, then grabbed at it with a move fast and surprising in its ferocity. I swore Shorty was going to deck him. I imagined the case was about to be complicated by a courtroom riot. Shorty jerked his head back and ran from the courtroom. We seldom saw Shorty take off his hat. It was part of his being, as much as the ears attached to his head.

"You will sit down if I tell you to sit down!" the bailiff commanded as he spun back around to face Woody.

Woody was terrified. "But . . ."

"Sit down!"

The only seat was in the middle, a lone chair between a woman nourished on a diet of too much fatback, her thighs cascading over the sides, and a crank-gaunt man with crablike eyes. "I won't be responsible if I flip out," Woody stuttered. The bailiff was irritated; he kept pointing. Woody carefully sat down between the two people, eyes wide with fear.

Blackie was already seated in the corner near me. Shorty came back. "I couldn't leave my partner," he said. His hat was off. The bailiff glared. He sat down.

The judge went through the routine of explaining the court procedure to the crowd of the tattooed, unshaven, alcoholic. An interpreter droned quietly in Spanish.

It was a surprise that Blackie and Woody and Shorty were called first, as a trio, ahead of the accused murderers, rapists, and thieves. More surprising to the judge, it seemed, was the fact that they were even there. (When we had first arrived, the deputy at the desk scoffed when asked if they had yet shown, for he said they were transients and transients never made court dates.)

The men filed to the bench in front of the crowd of Broderick citizens who would likely resemble the jury of their peers. Blackie stood on the left with his hands crossed in front. Woody was next to him, his hands in imitation of Blackie, as if in church. Shorty took up the right, with his hands defiantly at his side.

"Each of you has been charged with creating a public nuisance," said the judge. "What is your plea to the allegation of December 15 that you created a public nuisance?" she asked Blackie.

"Not guilty, Your Honor."

Woody piped in out of turn, "And I'm not guilty either!"

Shorty nodded. I heard him say he needed a beer.

The judge didn't know what to say when they announced they were going to fight the order. The judge explained they would have to return to court on February 21. She asked if they could be in court on that date.

"I don't know if I'll be in this state!" Shorty said. The courtroom erupted in chuckles.

She patiently explained the procedure, and the three men agreed to the date.

"Your Honor," Blackie said. "Do you know what this is about, the homeless . . . ?"

The judge interrupted and told him explanations would have to wait until February. They were given a court-appointed attorney. The men stumbled out of the realm so foreign to them, to the bus, where they popped beers and told and retold every moment of their day in court. They were feeling good about things.

"Hey," Blackie said when we got back to camp, "we beat their fucking asses already, eh Dale? As long as there aren't no fucking complaints, there ain't no bullshit anymore."

Wе STOOD ON THE SHORE two days after the court appearance, watching the waterfall of the sewer plant across the river. Woody and Shorty were sitting on the bank with a line in the water. We always saw them fishing but never saw them catch a fish. Blackie was standing. We talked about the old days and modern days and what citizens imagine to be the essence of the hobo life. A lot of people think of *Emperor of the North Pole,* a popular 1973 movie set in the Depression, starring Ernest Borgnine as "Shack" and Lee Marvin as "A No. 1," the best hobo in all the land. The movie was a battle between the two men over a bet in the hobo jungle that "A No. 1" couldn't ride Shack's train.

"Phony as hell," Blackie said. "Fighting on top of a boxcar, goddamn. I'll stand on top of the son of a bitch. It gets goin' thirty or forty miles an hour, I sit down, take off my belt, and tie me on that fucker. The dumb fucks crawling through the train, crossing the couplings, never hanging on, never knowing when that son'bitch is going to slam. She slams, brother, you're gone. I seen guys get shot up, fall out of boxcar doors, all kinds of weird shit."

Blackie then said he hates riding trains. "Boring," Blackie proclaimed. We thought it odd that a hobo would say such a thing. The best part of being a hobo, Blackie explained, is not riding trains. It's leaving, getting there, until there gets to be a burden, and you repeat the process an unlimited number of times.

We looked up and saw Vera walking down the levee toward us. She had a jug, a gallon of white wine, a few mason jars for glasses. Vera poured herself a drink. Vera was steaming about Alice, whom she claimed was spreading stories about her having sex with all the men in camp. When Vera was finished spitting about how much she despised Alice, Woody put down his fishing pole.

"You missed me!" Woody said. He lowered his head and studied his line.

"Me too!" said Shorty.

"I don't think you got me either," Blackie said.

Vera topped off her mason jar. She offered some wine to Blackie. He declined and looked out at the river. Blackie had just been telling me how proud he was that he hadn't been drinking more than one beer every few days for several months. "I sit here with the same fucking beer for a half hour," he told me weeks earlier. "Sometimes longer. By the time I get through drinking it, it's piss warm." Vera again offered and Blackie said no. Vera drank. Oh what the hell, Blackie said.

She poured him half a quart jar of wine. He announced one drink wouldn't hurt. The jar was emptied in a matter of minutes. Vera again filled it.

We took off. I had to leave town on business. Michael came to the camp over the next week and gave reports via phone of a raging drunk. Wheelbarrow loads of wine bottles were being consumed. Blackie was drinking and dancing, doing the "Blackie jig." Luke later described it as "the top half of his torso is kind of like a Slinky, the bottom half is what makes it all jive together." When I came home, I saw enough myself.

The camp was in turmoil, and the binge peaked the very night I got home. I was anxious to find out what was going on, so we went down to the shore the following morning.

We arrived at 11:00 and Blackie was still in bed. He was doing something we'd never witnessed: hinting, almost begging, for a drink. There was a bitter north wind blowing. Michael photographed him in the shack, sitting on the edge of his bed, with the light streaming in through the window. Behind was the wall made of cardboard boxes, with the word *fragile* written on one box over his shoulder.

"I need a drink," he proclaimed.

His eyes were heavy. We went outside. Bill staggered from his tent. His hair was wild and long. Bill worked fast to get a fire going. Road Dog and Helga were sleeping in their tent.

Blackie emerged from his house. He shivered and said he needed a drink real, real bad. He hugged the edge of the new flames. He repeated again how he needed a drink real, real bad.

We went over to see Woody and Shorty at their camp. They were sitting around a fire built in a barrel. Woody had a beer in hand. Right after we walked up, Bill and Blackie came down the bank behind us.

Woody looked nervously at Bill, hanging back for a reason then unknown. It quickly became clear that Bill had offended Woody in some major way, for Woody picked up a heavy steel mallet. He placed it at his side when he sat back down on an inverted can near the fire.

"I'm ready," Woody said. "That's how you take care of family."

Bill was about twenty feet away. He slowly approached. Woody never took his eyes off him. Bill came up behind, stammering. He did not know about the mallet.

Woody was jumpy.

"Don't you get behind me."

Bill edged forward, put his hand on Woody's shoulder. Woody flinched.

Bill asked how it was going.

"What did I ever do to you?" Woody asked.

"Nuthin'."

Bill took off his glasses and showed the shiner Road Dog gave him last night. It was bright, the color of a mussel shell.

"What did you do?" Woody questioned.

"Nuthin'. I don't know why he done it."

"Can I buy a drink off you?" Bill inquired.

There was a pause as Woody looked down at the five cans left from the six pack at his feet.

"No, but I'll give you one."

Shorty figured it was a good time for a joke. He told one about a Navajo Indian who went to the war and didn't speak any English. He was with the Marines, and there was a huge battle, with bombs and bullets flying. The Indian ran like hell with shrapnel exploding all around him and dove into a foxhole with a Marine from New York. The New Yorker was stunned that the Indian had braved the battle to move forward. He tried to speak English but quickly learned the Indian didn't understand. So he went for sign language. He ran his fingers down his arms, to signal the falling bombs. "Ugh," said the Indian. Then the New Yorker thrust his fist in the air, to signify when it quieted down, they'd stick their heads up. "Ugh," said the Indian. Then he put his hands to his eyes and made rings with his fingers, and moved them in and out to signify they would look around and see if the coast was clear.

The Indian's eyes widened. "Ugh!" he screamed, and he leaped from the foxhole. Bombs barely missed him as he ran to a nearby foxhole, where there was another Navajo Indian.

The Indian was amazed he'd run from his safe shelter.

"Why the hell did you do that, man?" the other Indian asked.

"That crazy white man told me in sign language when the bombs fall down and night comes," the Navajo said, running his fingers down his arm like the white man did, "he was going to fuck me." He then thrust his fist in the air like the white man did and said: "until my eyes bugged out!"

Shorty formed his fingers in rings that he moved in and out from his eyes. Everyone laughed. Everyone but Blackie was drinking. Booze started whatever happened last night, and booze ended it.

Woody gave Blackie a beer.

"I got my wish!" he said, drinking deeply.

After we left that morning, Bill moved on, to dry out at a detox center in another city. Herbert skipped that day as well, to San Francisco. He had bought a round trip ticket, to be gone four days, but Blackie wasn't looking for him to come back.

"He took me for twenty and Road Dog for thirty," said Blackie. It turns out Herbert was not what he seemed. He also lifted some food stamps off another group in a nearby shack. Herbert was quiet, but when the drinking started, he changed. He began eyeing Helga, Helga was eyeing him back, and tension grew with Road Dog over this matter. Anyway, Road Dog's patience was being taxed enough as it was. We learned the reason he'd punched Bill was because Bill had thrown a whole can of diesel on the fire and almost burned them all up. It was good they weren't too drunk to have jumped back in time before it exploded in a big ball of flames. Both Bill's and Herbert's departures were opportune.

Road Dog also moved out. He'd come back into the camp after the sweep, but now as things were going, he feared the cops coming by surprise. He couldn't afford to meet them. He used Helga's welfare money to get a room at the Stardust Motel—which rented by the week or month and seldom by the night—on the avenue about a mile and a half from the camp.

The binge was like a great crescendo to some finale, though the story was not over. When we came again in the second week of February, we drove up the dusty road and spotted Blackie walking on the tracks next to the rice mill. The mill was quiet for the first time—the cooperative that owned it had been forced by finances to sell to developers. Blackie walked slowly and seemed depressed. But he wouldn't talk about it. Not that we probed.

Blackie leaned on a wall, the sun in his face. We watched a stream of winos come out of a cement shack near the Tower Bridge. Blackie looked good, better than last week, but Jesus, anything was better than last week. The sun was breaking through the clouds, and you knew this day that spring was not far off, good riding weather. It was getting much warmer. Already the hobos were moving. I'd seen them in the jungle near the yard across the river and on trains.

Blackie didn't like being all alone and sober. Yet he wasn't seeking a drink. He looked back on the last two weeks and said he was glad to be rid of them.

Blackie headed off to wherever he was going, nowhere. We waved to Alice and Burt, whose van was parked on the levee about a hundred yards up from Blackie's Camp. Something was unusual: the van was running. Alice's son was playing cards with a guy we saw all the time who wore a "goober hat," with its brim rolled up, like a clown might wear. They played cards on a table of sorts between them that was a chewed-up piece of plywood set on two pails. Goober Hat was winning, and the son was frustrated. Things had escalated between Alice and Vera. Alice was fuming because Harry told her that Vera was asking to use his bus to push her van over the levee and into the river. Alice said Vera's anger stemmed from jealousy, believing that Alice was horning in on the attention of the guys.

While we talked about the ramifications of all this, Alice looked over at Fanny's trailer—the prostitute had moved it back after the police sweep and it was again parked near the Tower Bridge. Alice recounted a steady stream of johns who knocked at the door. When they came, the man who lived with her walked down to the bamboo thicket to sit and wait until she was done. Fanny, according to Alice, used to live in an old house where the big condo project was going up, but it was torn down when they started excavation. Fanny and her man then ended up at the river. Fanny had walked the avenue for a while, but she now had a clientele who came to her trailer.

"She had a baby last year, but the county took it away," said Alice. "It was born addicted. They sit on their step and shoot up right in plain sight. Anyone can see them."

We left Alice and Burt and passed Fanny's trailer. Moose followed. Fanny came out and offered a few hot dogs, and Moose bounded over to her. This was a woman who was once beautiful but now looked like a worn Barbie doll, with blackened eyes and a wasted frame. Her arms were severely black and blue from shooting up. Alice told us that Fanny's limp came from shooting up in the leg and that the doctors told Fanny she may lose it if she keeps sticking a needle in it.

Fanny smiled in a neighborly way, but she had cheerless eyes, which looked into you with a combination of boredom, sadness, hate. She staggered on her swollen leg back into her trailer.

The whole of Broderick was a soap opera. Red, who first turned me on to Blackie, was bitten up by a police dog a week earlier after he'd pistol whipped his girlfriend. He took seventeen stitches. Blackie was different from these Broderick people. I think he would still prefer living on the Sacramento side of the river if not for the police. He was camped over there when Bronco Billy was raiding homeless camps by night, burning them up and throwing people's gear into the river.

We turned around. As we again passed Fanny's trailer-shack, a car came at us. It was a low-riding cruiser with old-style black California plates. Two *guarros* were in the car. One was a big fat man, and he waited outside with his arms crossed while the thin man went inside. We surmised they were delivering the white powder that was Fanny's salvation. The *guarros* were mean looking, and we edged away from them as discreetly as possible.

I came back alone one evening not long after; it was beyond dusk, almost full dark. I stood on top of the levee, trying to see if a light burned in camp through the trees. I edged down the path. The camp was dark. I sensed Blackie was in his house, but knocking wasn't the right thing to do.

I returned to the top of the levee and studied the stars, the ones visible at that hour. Those of us who live in houses do not really see the night sky the same way a person without a home does. We mostly see it in pieces, while passing between automobiles and buildings. (I was about to drive back to my house with electric lights and stereo music that would deprive me of exposure to the real world of the dark.) The sky is a terrifying thing to view night after night. The longest I have done this was for better than a one-month stretch, when I walked alone across the Utah desert at age nineteen. I came away from that experience believing that if a law could be passed mandating that the roofs be torn from all of our homes and replaced with glass bubbles, our society would be better for it. We would constantly be reminded of the important things and not go on with our petty and sometimes cruel ways, thinking as we do that we will go on living forever, that there are no consequences for our actions against each other and the environment. If you have gone camping, think of the times you leaned back from a fire and studied the stars. Remember how you thought about infinity, which led to your thinking of death—the fact that we are all nothing more than submicrobes on a speck of sand arcing through inky space. I wonder how it would affect a person to lie beneath the cosmos hundreds of nights in a row, as does a hobo. Perhaps you get used to it. I doubt it. Blackie had gone to bed early and I wonder if he had done so to escape being alone with the stars, at an age when he was so close to the end of his life.

We are all alone, of course, but we can hide from it better than can a person who lives beneath the stars.

The Eskimos are supposed to have many names for different kinds of ice, be it mushy, dry, crystalline, or the grades between. There could be an equal number of names for the many distinct kinds of nights I saw at the camp. There were nights when the Tule fogs were thick and the mood closed and dark as a shuttered house; full-moon nights that turned to memories of youth and romance, before the decimating truth was learned; rainy nights that bore heavy on the memory of the dead; nights such as this, empty, sharp, small, in which a lone man inside the thin walls of a shack is bare and helpless against the universe of stars.

Dreams.

Somewhere in the insignificance of the night, The Dream has The Moment; but, as everyone knows, moments ultimately emerge into Reality and then night again falls and the cycle is renewed. But are they dreams or just words never spoken?

Blackie and the boys tried to meet with the public defender to discuss their case one week before the second court date, but the lawyer was never there when they called from a pay phone. Blackie figured they could argue a necessity defense, in the same way a starving person who steals an apple from a store to keep from dying might evade conviction.

I contemplated breaking our rule and writing a story—it was a good story for a newspaper—so after leaving repeated messages, I talked with the public defender, who didn't say much and seemed disinterested, as well as with a local public interest attorney. The second attorney felt a necessity defense would not work but that the men could argue prevailing standards. That is, were the police unequally enforcing the law in the city of West Sacramento, singling out River People while ignoring other crimes?

While I grew more keen on the legal fine points of the case, even though I chose not to write the story, the camp continued to swirl with change.

The biggest news was the breakup of the partnership between Woody and Shorty. Shorty said Woody was making him do all the work. Woody was used to being taken care of ever since they had first met, when Woody had the two broken legs, Shorty said. Shorty grew tired of waiting on him now that Woody was again healthy. We never heard Woody's version. Woody had hooked up with Harry, who drove his bus to some distant location. Shorty moved into Herbert's house, and he fixed some of the disrepair the camp had fallen into.

Blackie spent most of his time sitting quietly. Martin, the former steelworker, was bringing food and wood, and it was this largess that kept Blackie going. He was quiet in a way I had never seen, but I figured it was just a phase.

At this time, the mysterious woman moved closer into the circle and we actually spoke a few words with her, though she would not say much about herself other than that she had a home and came only to walk the two dogs.

Luke also moved into the camp, sleeping in Bill's old tent. He was more eager than ever to learn how to become a hobo. Shorty and Blackie were going to teach him, and this helped take the focus off of the court appearance by giving everyone something to talk about.

Luke would go on about what kind of hobo he wanted to be—just like Blackie. "To me, he's like a Jesse James legend," Luke said. "Well, I mean the positive." He got Blackie to tell a few stories, but Blackie told them without gusto.

The police were apparently not at all happy with the court fight. Shorty said Sgt. G. H. Walker, a sidekick to Sgt. Wilson, stopped him walking down the avenue. Shorty had a paper bag containing two quart bottles of beer. "Let me see that bag," Shorty quoted Sgt. Walker as saying, and when the sergeant took the bag, it fell from his hands, shattering the bottles.

"Oops," he told Shorty.

A week after the beer-bottle incident, Alice told us she was standing in front of the big supermarket with a sign, "Will Work for Food." Sgt. Wilson was giving her trouble for this, but Alice proclaimed First Amendment rights. A few days later, a woman asked if Alice wanted some work, and the woman took her home to rake her yard. Alice was just about finished when a police cruiser pulled up front. It was Sgt. Wilson. She thought he had come to hassle her, but Sgt. Wilson was merely coming home to his wife.

The police, however, did not come near the camp during the time between the trials. More River People began to move back, and a few newcomers even showed up. Everybody was waiting to see what happened with the trial. There was a strong hope among Vera and Alice that the men would win. I think, though, that Blackie felt he was going to lose, in the way hobos always lose when they come up against the world they left. Now when we came to the camp, often Blackie would be at the Stardust Motel with Road Dog and Helga. We'd go there and find Blackie watching television. He talked about moving on with Road Dog to Sparks, Nevada, to take care of some business. Few people recycled there, and the town's trash bins were loaded with aluminum cans. Sparks was a mecca for canning—a person could make $20 to $30 a day pulling cans from the trash, which was a fortune by hobo standards. But Blackie's heart didn't seem to be in it. He looked like he wanted to sit on the bed and watch television for the rest of his life.

Because of the malaise, food was in short supply at camp. With the exception of Shorty, no one was minding chores. Mister the cat had to be creative. One day, Shorty found Mister inside a pot of beans. Shorty's biggest concern was that the cat would stink him out of his shack that night—the cat had an odorous history. He shooed the bean-eating cat from the pot and tried the beans, but the cat fur was just too much, so he gave the rest to Moose, who would spend the night in the airspace of Blackie's chamber. As food got tighter, Shorty finally did catch some fish. Mister was desperately hungry as Shorty prepared the fish for dinner. Twice the cat tried to steal one. "You get one more warning, then you know what I'm going to do!" Shorty hollered. Mister again tried to swipe a fish. "That's it," Shorty said as he picked the cat up by the hind legs and flung it like a discus far out into the river. Moose tore into the water to rescue the cat. He tried to put his mouth around it to pull it in, but the cat managed to swim on its own. Shorty felt terrible for losing his temper. The cat ran back and jumped in Shorty's lap. He dried it off and warmed it with a towel.

On February 21, we followed the men to court. The excitement of the previous month was gone. Harry drove Woody to Broderick. He and Shorty were civil, though they were not exactly in a team spirit. Blackie's pessimism had even worn off on Vera and a few others who came. Shorty was still full of fight. They waited in the hall to meet the public defender for the first time. They never did get him on the phone. The judge was late, and the public defender was not to be seen.

"So she's on a piss call or coffee break," Blackie said of the judge, eager to get it over with. "Where's that fucking bailiff at? That smart asshole."

The public defender finally came. He called the men "mister" in the way a guy in a three-piece suit uses that word on men in soiled clothes, not as a title of honor, but with a combination of contempt (oh God, why didn't I get that big-time job with a big city firm!), fear (better be nice, they could make a scene), and duty. He said his words slowly, and many were three syllables, which instantly agitated Shorty. The public defender talked slower than usual, like someone speaking English to a foreigner would speak louder to make them understand. The attorney seemed tired.

All three men talked at once. "I got a fishing license," Shorty said. "They can do anything they want. I ain't guilty," said Woody. Blackie talked about the levee being federal flood control land. The public defender held up his hands and then noticed Michael's camera. He told the men they had to speak in private. We were not allowed in the meeting. I was very sorry at that moment I had not broken our rule and written a story, for there was no heat on. The men were going into this cold. I smelled a bad deal going down.

Michael and I paced the hall for over a half hour. When the door to the room burst open, Shorty was first out. He was waving his arms.

"They said they wanted to make a deal, probation for one year. I'm not going for that horseshit. He done pissed me off. I'm not taking no year's probation. I'm not moving off the river!"

Shorty sneered at the door where the attorney was standing. His head snapped between the door and us as he talked. "I'm not moving off that river!"

"I want a jury trial," said Woody. "I'll let twelve peers decide whether I'm guilty or not!"

Blackie said nothing. The public defender went to talk with the prosecutor. I got a strong sense that the last thing the new city of West Sacramento wanted was to spend all the money it would take for a jury trial for three men on a misdemeanor charge of creating a public nuisance, for the city had no shortage of murderers and rapists in need of prosecution. And I'm sure they didn't want the publicity that would get out, because I was now ready to write a story, rule or no rule. If I didn't, others would.

The public defender returned and began a carefully rehearsed talk. He told the men that if they wanted a jury trial, they would not be able to get it until fall—that meant staying around for at least another six months, if not longer. He said the *six* in a way that stretched it out to two syllables.

Shorty was getting ready to head to New Jersey. Blackie was tired. Woody didn't want to be around Shorty any longer—he just wanted to move on. None of the men desired an endless series of court dates in a game rigged against them. The public defender played off these concerns. Finally, the men agreed to the latest deal: all charges dropped if they would just leave the shore and promise not to camp there again. The men filed into the courtroom. The judge said they would have one month, until March 23, to vacate the camp. She concluded by asking if they had any other questions. They just looked at the floor.

"What's a hobo supposed to do?" Blackie asked as they left the courtroom.

W E'D GIVEN BLACKIE A COPY OF OUR FIRST BOOK, which he kept in his house on the library shelf with unsold portions of his special magazine collection. "Can I have one, too?" Luke asked one night while we were sitting around the fire, not long after the final court hearing.

"Sure," I said. "I'll bring one tomorrow."

"Could you wait," Luke said, "could you wait until May 7?"

I asked why.

"Because that's my birthday. I want to get it on my birthday."

I made a promise.

"Could you sign it before you give it to me?"

I promised.

"And could you maybe wrap it?"

Of course, I said. He wanted the book, he said, because of all the pictures of hobos. He talked about hitting the rails once he got his federal disability money.

Since Woody left, Luke had been working on Shorty to become his partner. Blackie and Shorty accepted him into the fold, not quite all the way, but enough so that he became at least a part-time member. Blackie seemed a little put off by him at times, for he was occupied with other thoughts—he sometimes grew frustrated with Luke and these were the only times we ever saw him angry—yet at other times he was very kind.

Shorty was set to ride the rails himself. He'd recently found a fine pack in a trash bin, a road pack with a metal frame. Shorty had the hobo luck—hobo luck was finding a twenty in the gutter when you were at your brokest and most hungry, or having a woman pick you up hitchhiking and take you home in your greatest time of spiritual and physical need. Luke had bought a pack, and Shorty helped him get other gear. We saw Shorty increasingly fussing over Luke's interests. One day, Shorty and Blackie dressed Luke up with all his gear so he could see how he looked as a real hobo. Luke was proud. "I'm going to be a hobo!" he exclaimed.

But as March wore on, it became a surprise to see Blackie at his house any longer. Blackie was more often found at the Stardust Motel with Road Dog and Helga, where a collection of shampoo bottles and other toiletries and boxes of food had grown to crowd the window ledges. Shorty and

Luke kept up Blackie's house, and no one dared move in. Blackie was always engrossed in the television at the Stardust, lying on the floor or the bed. Moose vanished in this period, and this furthered Blackie's depression. Several times, the dog had broken away from the Stardust and had roamed back to the camp empty of people. Blackie would take Moose back to the hotel. When Moose disappeared the last time, Blackie let on that he was lost. I didn't know what really happened until much later—Blackie had given the dog away to a friend. Moose had been the closest living creature in the world to Blackie.

The day before the camp was to be shut down, as ordered by the decree of the court, Martin came, and Blackie and the boys gathered up all their aluminum pots and a few batteries they had found, to take them in Martin's truck to sell for salvage. Shorty was fussy, though. He kept the camp's appearance up as if it was going to go on forever.

That night, we went to Alice and Burt's camp. They were tearing it down in preparation for burning.

"Better us to burn it than to let them," Alice said.

Blackie was there. "Road Dog and Helga got drunker than fuck last night," he said. "They drank four six packs." Blackie was not drinking to get drunk these days. He said this and then did not talk with anyone—he sat twenty feet away from the group. Alice and Burt lit the pile of wood, chairs, and other debris. The flames rose to ten feet. A hobo named Tennessee said hell, might as well make use of the fire. He broke out some hot dogs to roast over the flames. There was a grand sky that night, and the River People were silhouetted against the last red of the sun flaring from behind the distant Coast Range.

Someone asked Alice if she was worried the flames would attract the police.

"Let 'em come. What are they gonna do, throw us out?"

The fire burned down to coals that radiated powerful heat. The figures around it were quiet shadows against the emerging stars. I don't remember all of what was said, but there was not much conversation. Talking seemed wrong, and everyone sensed this. I remember a lot of time passed. Slowly, the spiritlike forms shambled off to different corners of the night.

That was the last time we saw Blackie at the shore. When we went to the camp the next day, no one was there. We sat all afternoon, until full dark. We told ourselves we were waiting for the cops (they had not come that morning when Shorty and Luke saddled up and walked off), but we were half hoping Blackie would show up one last time. The camp was cleaner than we had ever seen it. Shorty had raked and swept the dirt down to hard mineral soil, neatened everything up, as if to make the camp an attractive corpse. There was not even a stray leaf left on the ground.

We left the camp at dark and went to the Stardust. Luke was sitting on a chair near the door. Blackie was on the floor watching a Cheech and Chong movie. Road Dog and Helga shared a bed. In spite of the room's warmth, Helga had a blanket pulled up around her. She had recently lost her baby.

"I call him Papa," Helga said of Blackie. Blackie paid no mind, for he was seriously into the movie. Helga and Road Dog then talked to Luke as adults would talk to a child in their midst. Luke jabbered about hopping a train to Oregon.

Helga, who was at the front end of a big drunk, shook her head.

"You see the good part of it, Luke, not the rough part," she said. She talked loudly, her eyes furrowed. "There's stabbings. Luke, you've never really seen the bad. These guys are pros, and he's been stabbed," she said, pointing to Road Dog next to her on the bed.

"I knew the guy nine years and he stabbed me," said Road Dog, who lifted his shirt and showed a lightning bolt of a scar. "He wanted my stamps. He knew I had $200 coming in."

Helga nodded. "Luke, you were lucky. You went into a friendly camp. Pop's camp is friendly."

All the while, Luke was looking down, feeling scolded. He just wanted to be a good hobo. Luke went to the bathroom.

"He goes in and out," said Road Dog. "He's even got a hobo name. Tinker. That's 'cuz he is always sittin' like this."

Road Dog demonstrated by putting his hand under his chin, like Auguste Rodin's *The Thinker*. "'Cuz he's not all there, he can't be a thinker. He's a tinker."

Luke came back into the room. When Luke got back from Oregon, he planned to live with Helga in an apartment that Road Dog was going to set her up in across the river, until Blackie and Road Dog returned from Sparks. The two men were set to leave after some check came on April 5.

"Road Dog is gonna come back," Helga said, nudging him.

"I keep my word," he said.

We spent several hours at the Stardust that night and Blackie said nothing in the time I was in the room.

I left with Luke in the middle of our visit to get coffee at a nearby hash house. It was a chilly night. I could see Luke's breath as we walked.

"Him, in my opinion, I consider him like the dad I never had," Luke said of Blackie. "Or the mom I would've like to have had."

Luke was eager to ride a train with Blackie.

"He's gonna be gone for a month, and then he's gonna be back here the first half week of July," Luke said. "Then he says, 'I'll come down here and see if you have your stuff together, I'm taking off for Montana, and then from there, hooking it on the main line back to Iowa.' Without a doubt, the number one person to travel with would be Blackie."

I didn't tell Luke that Blackie also said he was going to ride with us to the hobo convention. Luke wasn't clear on Blackie's plans. "Would you do me this favor," he asked as we ordered our coffee, "would you ask him when you get back, I don't understand what's going on with his travels."

I had never heard Luke's story. We sat in a booth. Luke told me he was born in Spokane, Washington, thirty-five years earlier. He'd been homeless more than half of his life.

"A little over a year after my mother and sister died in a car accident, my dad remarried to, for all intents and purposes, I would say, the step-witch. When the accident happened, I was just getting out of grade school. I repeated a year in grade school, so I was thirteen years old at the time of the accident."

Luke told tales of repression and how the new wife put down his mother. Luke bucked hay and did yard labor, to earn money and to avoid the house.

"The thing I resented most, she put my mother and sister down, that was burning a definite bridge for me. After my dad remarried this gal, I lived under the roof for I think a total of three years. It just got to the point where I got tired of it. My dad set me down and said, 'Look, this is the way it's going to go. You either go along with the program, or there's the door.' And I said, 'Fine, I made up my mind a long time ago. But,' I says, 'before I hit that door, old man, I want what I've earned.' I wanted some of my savings money. Shit, it was only a couple hundred dollars, you know. And he says, 'uh-uh, it's in a joint account. You can't touch that bastard until you are twenty-two years old.' I says, 'I worked for it as a man, I want it as a man, and I want it right now.' So we battled, we exchanged for a while. I snuck out in the middle of the night with just the clothes on my back. I hitchhiked in knee-deep snow back into Spokane, walked most of the way, spent all but $2 for a bus ticket to Seattle."

Luke slept in the Seattle bus station the next night. Then he met a guy in the station who took him in, a short order cook who said he helped runaways. Luke lived in a flop with the man, doing odd jobs. He couldn't get real work, because he was underage. When he turned seventeen, the man suggested he join the military. That was in 1972.

Luke enlisted. He said he had no trouble shooting a rifle and throwing grenades. But he had all kinds of problems with mechanical things. One time, the machine gun jammed and the drill sergeant screamed that he wouldn't last one day in Vietnam. Luke swore at the sergeant and got in big trouble.

"I went in there very rebellious. I went through three different drill sergeants. I got to the point where I had my times where I wanted to take my vacation, you know, and I'd go AWOL off the base, fuck around, do my thing. I'd get back and of course there was an Article 15 waiting for me. I guess I was a snot-nosed little punk kid that wasn't willing to be owned by the United States government. And I was still running away from personal problems."

Disciplinary action increased to the point where he was sent before the base commander. The commander gave him a stern lecture and one more chance. Luke failed and was returned to the office. "Unfortunately, son," Luke recalled him saying on his second visit, "Uncle Sam cannot afford the tab, to put it bluntly, to keep you in our weaponry training and in our mechanical training. You have a hard time grasping in a short period of time."

Luke was discharged as unsuitable for military life. "The only thing I didn't like is I couldn't keep my uniform. This was the first time I ever liked a suit in my life."

Luke said he went back to Spokane for six months, working and living in a local rescue mission. His trouble continued. Luke said it was just like the army—it was as if the men were owned by the mission's staff workers, who acted like lords. One day, he chewed out the mission director.

"I says, 'look, goddangit, what makes you think you're any better than these fellows out here? Let me tell you something, sir, I learned a hell of a friggin' lesson, and I'll tell you exactly what I've learned. I'll lay down any day with these fellas instead of you fucking pricks, because you're nothing but a lying motherfucker calling yourself a Christian soldier. God's gonna get you one day for that, sir.'"

He was promptly fired. Luke hit the road with a guy in the mission.

"We got a bus ticket to Missoula, Montana. He stole a car. I didn't know the first thing about theftin' a car. I didn't want to know. We went up to Great Falls, robbed a few cash boxes and business places, traveled with the car all the way from Great Falls, Montana, down a north-south route, finally ended up in Phoenix, Arizona."

He dumped the man there. He didn't like having a partner like that. For the next decade and a half, Luke roamed the West alone, never traveling with anyone. Except for an occasional period where he got general assistance welfare for single men, he never received any help. By the time he came to this shore, Luke had been on the road eighteen years. He never went back to see his father; he didn't even know if he was still alive.

"I have mental health problems," Luke said. "Most of this is based on . . . what it is, I missed my mother and sister very much, and there are times my attitude and my character and my personality gets where I don't give a hoot, and I'll just go off the deep end, and I'll flip out. I don't like being around large groups of people. I mean, a small handful of people that I get to know, I don't mind, but as far as being around large groups of people, that's when I get very nervous, edgy, paranoid."

We returned to the hotel where everyone was silent and watching the television.

April came, good riding weather. Michael kept going back to the hotel, each time figuring it was the last he would see of Blackie until he returned from Nevada. One night well into the first week of the month, Michael sensed the guys were really leaving, even though there was vagueness to their plans.

"I tell you what," Michael said to Blackie. "I want to know you're okay, so I'm going to give you a quarter." With great theatrics, Michael dug the quarter out of his pocket. Blackie was sitting on the floor, wearing bifocals he had found in a trash bin. Michael set the quarter on the nightstand. "Now there's no excuse not to call."

Helga laughed.

"You just threw a quarter away," she said, chortling. "The best you can hope for is he buys a newspaper with that quarter. You know hobos don't call, don't check in. That's not the hobo way."

FOUR DAYS AFTER BLACKIE FINALLY LEFT, MICHAEL AND I WERE FEELING ROTTEN. Things had reached a nadir at work. We'd gone to the camp a few times, but it just made us sadder. We found out Shorty was still sleeping there, and so we left a note that we wanted to meet and have dinner.

We got to the camp in the day's last light. Shorty showed up when it was full dark. We built up the fire. Michael blew on the flames, and I carefully stacked on wood. The mosquitoes were thick.

Somebody had shattered Blackie's door by kicking it in.

"Well, Blackie, here goes your door," Shorty said as he wrenched the last splinters free from the hinges. He broke apart the door for the fire.

"Everybody took off," Shorty said. "There ain't nobody around to talk to no more. Right now, I just feel lost, because all my friends are gone. You turn around, where they at? Everybody else got cold feet and left. There's only one stupid little fool around. Me. I know if I get caught on this river, especially camping on this river, I know I'm going to jail for six months. I'm not worried about it. I don't stay around during the day. I get up at 5:30, 6:00 in the morning and I haul tail. You'll only catch me down here at night."

We talked about Blackie. "I don't know where they went in Sparks," said Shorty. There was a long pause. The crickets and night bugs were as loud as an argument. Shorty said that near the end, Blackie was bored to sickness with the hotel room. He spent nearly a month living there watching television. He didn't have the energy to hobo up to Sparks. He drove with Road Dog in an old station wagon they bought for $100. It was an ignoble way for a hobo to leave a town.

Shorty was eager for a new partner.

"I always travel in pairs. 'Cuz if you take notice, you see one hobo, you see another beside him, because one's watching each other's back. Yep." But Luke was not going to be his new partner. "Luke's all right. But it's his mouth. If he don't get his own way, he whimpers and cries. Runs his mouth too much. Everyone's been telling him to shut up, shut up, shut up, and he won't keep his mouth shut. How many times have you heard people tell him, 'shut up and sit there and listen—you'll learn by listening?'"

In the meantime, Shorty had a brief encounter with female companionship. He'd met a woman in a Broderick bar. They spent a night together, and by his account a fine time was had by all.

"I told her if I don't come on up tonight, I'll see you Tuesday. I wasn't with no other girl. I just got drunk and stayed on the river. I can't sleep with no walls around me. I left my backpack layin' up against the wall. When I come in Tuesday morning, I say where's my shit? She said I threw it in a Dumpster. 'You stupid bitch,' I said, 'if you were a man I'd kill you!' Everything I owned, all my clothes, my food, a couple cans of baked beans, coffee, some sugar, my bedroll, my washrag, my soap, my towel; everything went. The only thing I was left with were the clothes on my back. Martin give me another sleeping bag. Vera's gonna fix the zipper, 'cuz it's broke.

"I come and go as I please. I answer to no man, woman, or child. I answer to just one man alone, and that's the Lord above. Yeah, I felt like killing the bitch. Then I thought, hey, I found it in a Dumpster, and it ended up back in a Dumpster, what the hell," he added, finding an order in this, affirming the truth that the only true socialists (or perhaps antimaterialists) in America are hobos.

In the coming days, Shorty hung on at the camp. Whoever was smashing apart the camp was doing it by degrees. First it was Blackie's door. Then a board here. A stone there. One day, the porch was torn off Blackie's house. Another day, Shorty came back and his house had been smashed down, so that it was like an A-frame, with one wall still standing and the roof tilted at a wild angle. He slept inside the nook that was left without trying to fix it.

When May 7 came, we didn't forget our promise to Luke. Shorty told us Luke had caught a freight out with a stranger. He hadn't been around in weeks. In spite of this, we signed a book and wrapped it. A visiting friend, Michael, and I went down to the camp with a six pack of beer. We built up a fire and waited, telling stories to my friend about the heyday of the camp. The sun set. The beer was all used up.

"Guess we better go. Guess Luke's not going to make it," I said.

As I spoke, there was a crashing in the brush.

"I knew they'd be here!" Luke said breathlessly, running from out of the weeds. "I knew it!"

The stranger was with him. Luke explained they had just jumped off a moving train that had come down from Reno. Luke knew that was dangerous, that even experienced hobos hate getting off on the fly, but this train was not going to stop and he had to stop. The two men ran through the city and over the bridge to the west bank. His new friend thought it was a foolish exercise.

He said he didn't think we'd be waiting. I told Luke we had given up on him. I handed Luke his birthday present.

"I guess we all learned something about the meaning of friendship tonight," Luke said.

The camp continued to crumble from the effects of unknown hands. Shorty did something rare for a hobo: he got possessive. He wrote on the wall of Blackie's house:

> This is Blacke and Shorty Place.
> *So stay out.*

A few days later, this was written:

> Not any more.
> W.S.P.D.
> 5/16/90

Soon, Blackie's house was totally destroyed. The outhouse was tipped over, the water cooler gone, the round table flung into the river. Even Shorty gave up sleeping there. We never saw the West Sacramento Police Department come to enforce their order or officially take away the remains of the camp. The wreckage was left as if a monument or a message. Nearly three years later as I write this, some debris remains. Once in a while, a rubber tramp—a man in a car—sleeps on the site, one of the few people who camps on the shore these days. In the order of things, a camp is never owned and it never dies.

S EVERAL YEARS PASSED. Helga was right—Blackie never called. He never came back. A few months after he and Road Dog left, Michael received a message at work that Road Dog had phoned. The person who took the note wrote "Blackie is okay." There was no other information, no phone number. I later learned Road Dog had come back to town to live with Helga, that he and Blackie had parted ways in Sparks.

That was the last word we heard.

All along, we fully expected Blackie one day would show up back in the camp, as soon as the heat was off, perhaps to rebuild his house. That first winter, we went often to the shore to see if he'd returned. I also kept an eye on old street people around town, as well as when I was in Portland, Oregon, or in Los Angeles. I went to Santa Barbara and checked with long-time denizens Crazy Red and Regular Red. They had not seen Blackie, so he hadn't returned to his old stomping ground. Everywhere, I spotted men who walked and looked like Blackie, but when I neared they were always someone else. Both Michael and I carefully watched hobos we saw on passing freight trains. I asked hobos coming north and going south. None knew what happened.

In the meantime, on the first anniversary of the camp's demise, Michael and I went down to the shore. Someone had carted off the plywood from Blackie's house, and it was stacked upriver at the site of some fresh gravelike square excavations. Anchored offshore was a rusting hulk of a tug, flying a black pirate's flag, with a skull and crossbones on it.

The condominium and hotel development was stalled. The man who headed it up died, and the project was in limbo. Everything was overgrown and the riverfront mostly unpeopled, except for a bent woman who walked among the weeds near the bamboo patch, picking up aluminum cans. She had just a few, clutched like prizes.

Shorty's house, well, the one that was really Herbert's so long ago, was still half standing. The outhouse still lay on its side, and part of the oven made from blocks was holding out. It was a ghost camp. If we did not know what events had passed on this site, our imaginations would have run wild, much like they did on finding a ghost camp like this in the hobo jungle of Little Rock, Arkansas, many years ago.

As for the former residents of the camp, we ran into Luke and Shorty a few times. Some months after his birthday, Luke called because he had lost a picture of him with the guys that Michael had taken. We met at the shore. Luke was glum.

"Too much sentimental value to come here," Luke said.

He did not come here, he told us, even though he was then living in a Broderick house not far away. Luke had gotten his disability, but the social worker made him have a payee, a responsible person who could ensure he spent his money wisely, according to government policy. The qualifications to be a payee seem to be as follows: you have to live under a roof that the post office will deliver mail to and you have to be able to sign a check, or at least reasonably scribble an "X." Luke rented a room for $200 a month from his payee, who thought a wise way for Luke to spend his money would be to loan this man's family $1,600. With no receipt. Luke had lived in the house for six months, and now the payee was balking at paying him back.

It was near dark and Luke said he had to leave, or at least get away from the camp. We walked down the levee toward his payee's house. Luke could not stand the house. The favorite pastime of the family was shouting. They argued with such relish that it could be called sport-screaming. If it wasn't the wife screaming at the children, it was the wife screaming at the husband. When the wife slacked off, the husband took over. When the parents were gone, the children carried the weight. The husband sometimes screamed solo.

To escape, Luke said he would steal away with his sleeping bag to bedroll under the sky in a nearby field. After all the years living outside, it was hard being in a house.

I ran into Shorty twice. The first time I was riding a bicycle and he was crossing the street; we had a grand reunion in the center of the road. Shorty told me he rode a train to Salt Lake City and spent the summer in Utah after the camp broke up. He was then living in a back room of the hobo bar, doing "swopping," cleaning up after closing hour for his keep.

Shorty's latest trouble came when he was down on the Sacramento side of the river rolling a joint. He was rolling away and the two guys who were supposed to be keeping watch fell down on the job, for he looked and saw two shiny black shoes. As his eyes rose, he saw the blue pants, and then the badge. The cop shook his head and wrote him up. After he handed him the citation, the cop asked for the marijuana. "Aw, can't I keep it?" Shorty asked. "I'm busted anyway." The cop took it. "You can try," he explained.

Shorty talked about the camp in emotional terms. It was special, he said, and he missed the guys and he missed our visits.

The second time I saw Shorty was almost three years after the camp's death. I found him at the bar. His eyes were flat—he looked very tired. Like Luke, he'd gotten SSI disability and was forced to rent an apartment as a condition of getting it. (Luke was then renting a room above his in a building on the Sacramento side of the river.) Luke was still eager to be a good hobo and was still trying to get Shorty to be his partner. Shorty had a payee who was not ripping him off, but the walls were closing in and the cops were giving him big hassles. He was ready to dump it all and hit the hobo road—without Luke.

"I really miss the camp," Shorty said. "Sometimes I still go over there and sleep."

Woody, he said, was living on the river at a different place. Harry, who had the bus, died. Shorty had no word on Blackie. If Blackie had come through town, Shorty said he would have heard.

Blackie's fate troubled us. We worked all possible channels to find him.

I heard a rumor that he died in Sacramento, but it proved untrue, according to official records.

One night I rode my bicycle over to the Union Pacific railyard. I found three hobos waiting for a northbound, and when I asked if any of them knew Blackie, one man's eyes rose. He excitedly told me that Blackie had shot a man dead on 17th Street in Denver, right about the time he and Road Dog separated. But a check with the Denver police proved that rumor untrue as well.

The rumors were taxing. I worked other avenues, such as calling soup kitchens in Montana, another likely destination. I went to Loaves and Fishes, a Sacramento organization that feeds several hundred poor people each day, and they put an announcement over the loudspeaker. King David, who once rode with Blackie out of Spokane, came forward but had not seen him in several years. I ran into a fellow at the gate who looked just like Road Dog—I swore it was him—but the man threw up his hands and shouted, "I don't look like no one," then walked away.

I kept going to the railyard. As Blackie once said, The Word travels fast in the hobo world. In an age when telephones and FAX machines have brought instant communication to the citizen world, The Word among hobos is still equally effective, if only slightly slower. Yet there was no word.

Our best bet seemed to be the National Hobo Convention, held each August in Iowa. While the convention draws yuppie hobos, some real hobos still attend. Blackie always made a point to go. Michael went in 1991 and heard that Blackie rode in on a train the previous year, right after he split up with Road Dog. Michael went again in 1992, when Blackie would have been nearly eighty years old. He placed "wanted" posters around the convention. Michael found Reno Jack, who worked in a Dubuque, Iowa, mission; Reno Jack put Blackie up after the 1990 convention. Blackie was traveling with two men and a dog. Reno Jack told Michael that Blackie was very tired—he had never seen Blackie so somber. Blackie told him it was hard to get around any more. "I've got a place to go," Blackie said to Reno Jack, but he did not reveal where that place was located.

"Maybe his spirit was broken down through means other than the road," said Reno Jack, who started riding the rails after he served in the Korean War. Reno Jack said a lot of old hobos retire and don't want anyone to know. They hole up in a flop somewhere, which is an embarrassing situation, living death for a hobo. Reno Jack said when these guys catch the westbound—hobo talk for dying—no one ever knows.

I checked to see if Blackie had caught the westbound. I submitted requests to the vital statistics departments in all the Western states where Blackie was known to travel, as well as Iowa, because Reno Jack felt if Blackie was holing up, he was doing so in that state.

If Blackie died in Idaho, Iowa, or Montana, we will never know, because those states, in their desire to protect the privacy of the dead, lest we try to disturb their peace in the great beyond, forbid death records from being made known. The other states had no record of his death.

The friend who told me that Blackie had died in Sacramento came back with new information. A veteran hobo told my friend he knew an old man named Blackie who had been drowned on the west bank of the Sacramento River; he was killed by two men who fled to Reno, according to the man. This supposedly happened in 1990, the month uncertain. Death records show no such case, but if the body was not found, it could be true. The rumor, strictly hearsay, was as valid or off base as any of the others. I present it with all the others, even though I seriously doubt it, because everything about the fate of Blackie is hearsay. Rumor is all I have to offer.

Long ago, I promised to address the issue of choice, whether or not Blackie volunteered to become a hobo, or if life had forced him into a corner and he was making the best of the situation.

After getting to know Blackie over those months and with the passage of several years—ample time to witness and explore the topic—I do not have a simple answer. I come away from my friendship with Blackie with three views, complex and multipart, about this issue of "choice."

First, to argue against choice:

Maybe the choice was made for him, as a child, at a definable time as it was for Shorty when he was abandoned by his parents at age seven, or for Luke, when his mother died. For Blackie, maybe the Depression did it, or the wars. Maybe he was sent into descent by something unknown to us. Of course, I have not taken apart each step of Blackie's life to speak with authority. And if I did, it would not give me any more authority. This, after all, is not a work of fiction, and I cannot possibly pretend to place myself deep into his psyche. It is clear, however, that Blackie had a serious problem with alcohol, and something must have made him drink so heavily. I wonder how many times in his life he went over the edge, lost everything, hit the rails as a matter of having no options.

For the Murrays who lived nearby—this book contains a picture of their boys on the car seat on the beach below Blackie's Camp—are they future Blackies who will make a "choice" to become hobos? Blackie at one time looked just like the three-year-old boy whose dirty face stares at you from the page with those eyes that reflect Michael taking his picture. Many of us can see ourselves in the eyes of that little boy. We all start out wet, waxy, and equal, in theory at least, those first minutes from the womb, all facing the same odds of becoming a banker, a professor, a wino, or a drug addict. At age three, like this boy, we perhaps are still alike and equal. When do outside influences buoy or doom us? At age five, six, ten? This boy was already living in the weeds and had seen and felt things he should not. His course was being set. Hope may already have been taken from this boy, or he may yet have it, God willing. The part of me that argues against choice fears that someone will come along in seven decades to do a book about one of the Murray boys being the last great American hobo of his era. Even a hardened conservative who would look at Blackie and find plenty of fault cannot look at that Murray boy at age three and blame him for his condition, though fault may or may not be found with the parents. But could those same conservatives blame him seventy years hence if he becomes the Blackie of his generation?

A second argument, for choice:

Who says we all have to take part in a society in which money and material goods are the sole reward of a life? This goes back to the reality argument at the start of all this. You have a different view of America when it is framed by a boxcar door. Hobos call it the giant picture window on the world. Passing in front of you are the eternal suburbs, strip shopping centers, regional malls, the ubiquitous American flags flying tall over establishments selling hamburgers, automobiles, other merchandise. That is the America tucked at the back end of a cul-de-sac, two cars in the garage, sold in sixty-second increments, bought, plastic in hand, with nothing down, and once obtained, believed in as absolutely as religion. In that America, you are a something because you acquire objects and use them to make yourself up as you go along. In that America, you are programmed to follow a line that was laid out before you were born, a line that started the day Christopher Columbus set sail, for it was inevitable that the America he "discovered" was destined to turn out just the way it has. Columbus traveled a line that led directly from the Old

World to that dead-end street named after the daughter of a developer. You are born and pursue the line from Columbus to cul-de-sacs because the line is drawn and it must be followed. The hobo in the boxcar is a spectator on the other side of this illusion, who finds salvation in the form of a different line, the tracks that head toward the limitless horizon.

Hobos may be the vestiges of mountain men in our modern culture, people who just don't fit in. I believe anyone has the capacity to freely choose to become a hobo, and damn the psychobabble that dictates everyone who does not aspire to wealth is a victim abused by society.

A third, middle view on choice:

Assume I am a laborer, a factory hand now idled by the mills that have been shuttered at an alarming rate because of companies shipping jobs to Burma, leveraged buyouts, and so on. Mine was a well-paying job, and I am now forced to compete in a "service economy" in which the bulk of jobs pay one-third of what I was once earning. I have no other option but the "choice" to seek one of these low-wage service jobs, the kind of labor common to the last decade of this century. The curse of the nineteenth century was industrialization. The curse of our century is deindustrialization. There is plenty of competition for the jobs with declining wages. A friend tells me that thirty people called before 7:00 a.m. the day her husband's business ran an ad for a part-time janitor job. They lost count of the calls after that early hour. A person cannot live on the wages of such a job, but many do. If those of you earning well over $20 an hour dispute this, I dare you to try to raise a family on $4.25, $5, or even $6 an hour. I have met enough people who are working two minimum-wage jobs to know that I could not tolerate an existence of all work and no sleep just to eke out survival. If I did not have the skills needed to make more than a few bucks an hour, I might "choose" to become a hobo. While I would prefer to regain my factory job and make a decent living wage, lacking it, I could choose to live amid the counterculture of the hobo jungles. I would find more dignity in this and would certainly have a better quality of life, at least with regard to being a wage slave. I would not be choosing in a positive but in a negative sense—the lesser of evils.

Perhaps all three arguments are correct. Whatever the case, however, a hobo's life is harder these days, for reasons that should now be apparent. The older I get, the sadder our society makes me. We are intolerant in so many ways. I read that most American businesses now require prospective employees to urinate in a jar as a prerequisite for employment, as if it should matter that someone might opt to smoke a joint while relaxing over the weekend and it in no way affects his or her ability to work. (The test merely weeds out the stupid who do not stop taking drugs long enough to pass the test—and the test does not check for the most destructive drug of all, alcohol.) This might seem off the point, but more and more, we want to legislate lifestyle or dictate it through fiat. Why do we have to piss in bottles and why do we have to hassle hobos? Is there no room for a hobo in modern America? Why can't there be space for Blackie to build a house and live out his life in a traditional hobo way? The American West is still plenty big enough to give over a few weed patches near the railyards for their jungles.

Yet there are now hundreds of hut cities all across America, in New York, Chicago, Atlanta, even in places like Nashville. Much of what is recorded here about police harassment is not really any different from what now happens at least once each week all over America at other camps, such as the tunnel occupied by the "Mole People" in New York or the "City of Lost Souls" in Los Angeles. These camps continue to be broken up by authorities bent on enforcing the law, which, to paraphrase Anatole France, in its majestic equality prohibits both the rich and the poor from living in hut cities.

Enough of choice. Even if Blackie is a victim with no choice in the matter, he was beyond repair to ever become "normal" like us. If he was a broken part, he was firmly embedded in hobo life. His choice as an adult was that he did not want us to fix him.

When I first entered Blackie's Camp, I was researching a book project that for a variety of reasons went nowhere, about people dropping out to find new realities. In a minor way, a rebellion has taken place in this society against a period of alienation and personal emptiness. Much of this emptiness has resulted from an ethos of greed—as well as a level of cultural and corporate insensitivity—unparalleled in modern times. Many individuals have tried to find their own solutions. I came across a man who quit a job as vice president of a major bank to roast coffee beans, and I don't think he earned one-tenth of what he did previously; an IBM executive quit to join the Peace Corps; a Wall Street broker accustomed to huge sums of money became a gardener; a reporter went to Ireland to live in a cottage.

I pursued the project with vigor because I realized I was just like the people I wanted to write about. I had been growing more dissatisfied. The rats were coming out of my cellar in droves. I was writing books, which were my passion, but despite critical success, I was literally earning about as much from them as Blackie would make from selling the skin magazines he found in Dumpsters. I was making my living, a rather good one at that, with rewards of both financial and psychological income, from my day job at the newspaper in an industry that had grown incredibly more corporate and unsatisfying.

I fought them in all sorts of ways irrelevant here. My efforts were received in the way you greet a person holding a Bible at your front door. I learned the corporate world does not have the capacity to change. I had to change.

I rediscovered an essay by Leo Tolstoy, who, at the age of fifty-one, after having completed *War and Peace* and *Anna Karenina,* came into a dark period—his own career crisis of sorts. He questioned life and its meaning. In *Confession* (pp. 31–32), Tolstoy wrote

> There is an old Eastern fable about a traveler who was taken by surprise in the steppes by a raging wild beast. Trying to save himself from the beast, the traveler jumps into a dried-up well; but at the bottom of the well he sees a dragon with its jaws open wide, waiting to devour him. The unhappy man does not dare climb out for fear of being killed by the wild beast, and he does not dare jump to the bottom of the well for fear of being devoured by the dragon. So he grabs hold of a branch of a wild bush growing in the crevices of the well and clings to it. His arms grow weak, and he feels that soon he must fall prey to the death that awaits him on either side. Yet he still holds on, and while he is clinging to the branch he looks up to see two mice, one black and one white, evenly working their way around the branch of the bush he is hanging from, gnawing on it. Soon the bush will give way and break off, and he will fall into the jaws of the dragon. The traveler sees this and knows that he will surely die. But while he is still hanging there he looks around and sees some drops of honey on the leaves of the bush, and he stretches out his tongue and licks them. Thus I cling to the branch of life, knowing that inevitably the dragon of death is waiting, ready to tear me to pieces; and I cannot understand why this torment has befallen me. I try to suck the honey that once consoled me, but the honey is no longer sweet.

In this manner, many of us live. The honey has lost its appeal, but we are uncertain of which way to turn.

To take the question of choice to the ultimate test, I wondered if I could abandon the honey and confront the beast. I wondered if I myself could choose to become a hobo. It was, after all, one way out. I lost track of how many times Michael and I discussed this in the period of our troubles while sitting in Blackie's Camp. Michael said it frightened him just how much he was thinking about it. He said the biggest thing that stopped him was the boredom associated with the hobo life—so much time you sit around doing nothing but thinking. We believe at least half the petty arguments of Blackie's Camp were subconsciously induced to stir up some action among the men to fight their boredom. You can wait twelve hours for a train to come. If you have a camp like Blackie's, some days you can sit all day and do nothing but watch the river pass. There is enough monotony to drive you to cackling madness.

There was more stopping us, however. We lacked that something in us to do what Blackie did long ago. Whatever that something is, becoming a hobo goes far beyond dropping out. That something is part strength, part weakness, both pure freedom and an absolute prison. It is something terribly foreign, another reality that I, with my middle-class indoctrination, can never possibly understand, no matter how many freight trains I ride or how long I live on the edge of the homeless world. This is the most important thing I learned from Blackie. This is likely what I had been searching for in all the years I have written about poverty, and now that I know this, this likely will be the last book of nonfiction I write about the subject. In the extreme, I know that becoming a hobo for me would be an option I would take before I committed suicide, if things got so bad, but it would be its own form of death and rebirth. Michael grew up in poverty and understands it better than I, yet I believe he must be more of the citizen world than that of hobo reality. Otherwise, he would have taken Shorty's path.

The mysterious woman knew this about us long before we did. For months, she had been avoiding us, and when she eventually edged closer, she remained cautious. She was the only person associated with the camp who did not give unconditional acceptance. Near the end, Michael learned she had lived on the shore a long time before but now had a job and a house she owned. She let Michael know she was of the other reality, and it was clear she did not trust us around the guys because we did not live their reality. Michael went with her as she walked the two dogs, trying to convince the woman he understood because of his troubled background. The woman never bought it. We were interlopers, voyeurs, and perhaps exploiters who never could understand the shore.

After the camp was dead, Michael ran into the mysterious woman walking her dogs a few times. Michael's presence with the guys gone formed a truce of sorts, for it made her realize he was coming for reasons other than the ones she believed. On her penultimate visit, she roamed through the camp with great sadness. Yet she stuck to her story that she was only coming to walk her dogs.

The last time the woman came, Michael confronted her and told her he was there for the same reason she was: out of need. He said they were both looking for ghosts. She stood amid the camp crying. Michael hugged her briefly. She allowed this and said nothing. Then she left.

Michael went back a lot that first summer, often three times a day between photographic assignments. The woman never again came to walk her dogs. Michael went to the site of the camp more times than he wants to admit over the next year. Then he quit the newspaper and left town.

CASTLE
KALADONIA

—*a handwritten note
found at Blackie's Camp,
blowing in the wind
among the debris after his
house was destroyed.*

On an island not a far way away
I can see a *Kingdom Fantasy*
It comes complete with castle moat
Sometimes even a stream and a dragon

Castle Kaladonia does exist here
And dreams come true if you truly believe in yourself
Trust in magic to take your side to help you too
I was more than lost and scared when we met
You came to my rescue and swept me off my feet
I watched and enjoyed life

You took to the island and took me into your castle
I saw the doe and her fawn
The hummingbirds
Heard the owl
And learned

You enjoyed my happiness and shared in my island fantasy
Even when I talked of the dragon that watched over me
You never laughed or made me feel the insanity
And stood by my side
You even defended the moat dragon when others heard me

Thank you for a dream of life come true
For holding me as I would cry and being happy with me
You are special to me

You restored my faith and my trust in myself and showed me life
    through new exciting eyes of the love we share

What I want to say is if you ever need me I will be there instantly
With no questions asked
I'll be there

For the one thing you gave me is priceless
And no matter what I do I can never repay your support
You gave me my life again
Thanks
For my mickey moose T-shirt
cutoff jeans and barefoot magic knight of love

        Yours forever
        A damsel no longer in distress

THE
PHOTOGRAPHS

1
Graffito on the wall of the rice mill,
behind Blackie's Camp,
on the shore of the Sacramento River
in the town of West Sacramento.

2
Blackie's Camp, the center of a small city of sorts
for a group of hobos. Blackie's Camp had an oven, an outhouse,
a round table made from a giant wooden utility spool,
a water cooler, and a fire pit that was the center of social activity.

3
Blackie, a hobo dating to the 1930s, was hassled worse in the 1980s
than he'd been back in the Great Depression:
police sweeps had chased him out of several cities.
He fled to the west bank of the Sacramento River, building an
elaborate house that included a well-stocked kitchen.

4

Shoes next to Blackie's oven.

5

Wine bottles converted for use as water jugs.

6

*Blackie spent two days building his house from materials salvaged
from the shore, making it similar to a classic 1930s hobo design. The house
cost just $16, the price paid for the tarp that covered the roof.*

7

Blackie and Harry the cat.
Blackie surrounded himself with old hobo friends,
as well as a variety of animals.

8

Blackie's Camp was home mostly to veteran hobos,
but Blackie helped newcomers such as Luke; as a hobo-in-training,
one of Luke's duties was to cut firewood.

9

Shorty, a hobo friend of Blackie's who lived just downstream,
had to show Luke how to best cut firewood;
Luke didn't know it is difficult to saw through knots.

10
Blackie's dogs, Tie-Tie and Moose.

11

Blackie's neighbors immediately upriver did not build elaborate houses.
Burt came to the shore when his van broke down, with his wife, son, and Jaws,
a pitbull that often begged Burt to lower tree limbs
so it could hang by its teeth, sometimes for as long as 45 minutes.

12

Blackie was unhappy that many of his neighbors set up their camps
in plain sight, rather than hiding over the edge of the levee as he did—
being discreet was the proper hobo way to do things.

13

Blackie occasionally made social calls with his neighbors,
but generally avoided spending too much time in their camps.

14

Neighbors passed the time playing cards.

15

Store-bought cigarettes, neighbor's camp.

16

Burt's sixteen-year-old son with the family's new puppy.

17

Chair in Blackie's Camp.

18

Shorty's backpack.

19

*Tennessee, who lived temporarily in a house
built by one of Blackie's campmates,
cleaning his toenails with a homemade knife.*

20

The table outside Tennessee's house.

21

Luke, a thirty-five-year-old man mostly homeless since he was a teenager,
desperately wanted to be accepted by the old timers
so they would train him to be a hobo. Luke wanted to become
the best hobo in all the West. In the camp's early days, he often ran along the shore,
racing back and forth through the camp until he was exhausted.

22

Luke.

23

Luke with Moose after a run.

24

Shorty spent the first seven years of his life in a children's home.
He eventually married and had children, but heeded the call of the rails.
He celebrated his fiftieth birthday the year he lived at
Blackie's Camp and said he never planned to return to civilian life.

25

Shorty at the bathroom mirror.

26

The earring Shorty found in a Dumpster.

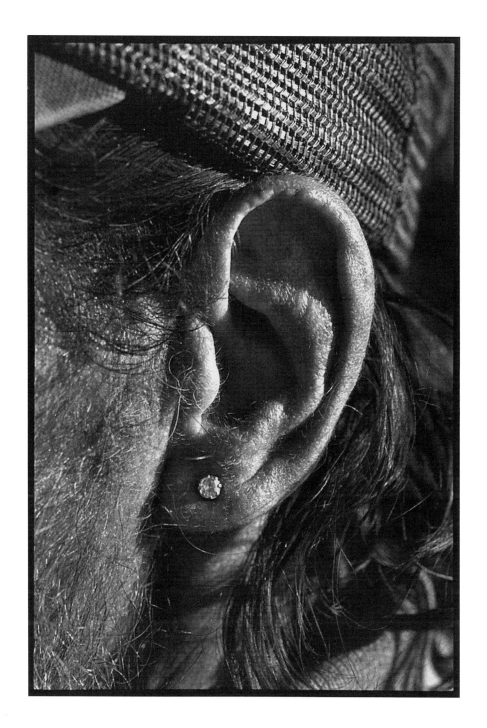

27
Shorty.

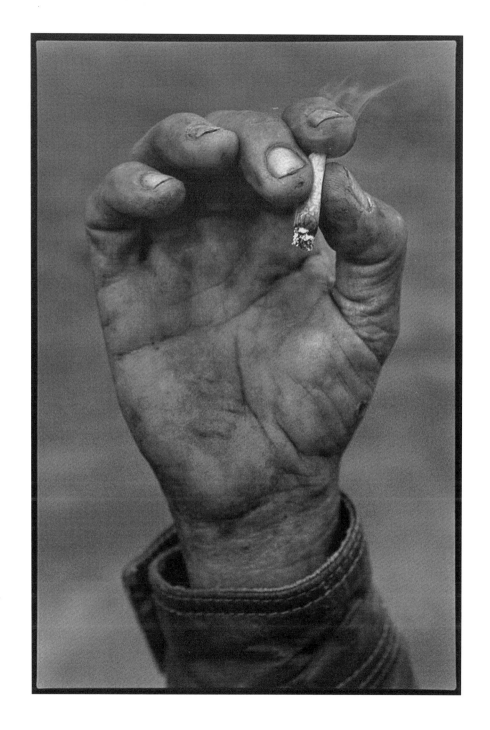

28

Blackie's skillets.

29
Striped bass caught by Shorty.

30
Shorty's fishing bait, kept high in a tree so it
would not be eaten by Mister, the hobo cat.

31

Mister got leftovers for dinner.

32

Freshly washed dishes.

33

An abandoned car downriver from Blackie's Camp, near the Murray's tent.
The car was a favorite playground for the Murray boys,
who arrived on the shore temporarily homeless with their mother and father,
an unemployed lumberman from the Pacific Northwest.

34

The Murray boys at the river's edge, on a seat taken from the stripped car near their camp. Blackie did not like the presence of children in the hobo jungle, for he said children brought the attention of authorities.

35

The Murray boys lived on the shore for several weeks.

One of the boys returned a dropped film canister.

36

The youngest Murray boy, age three.

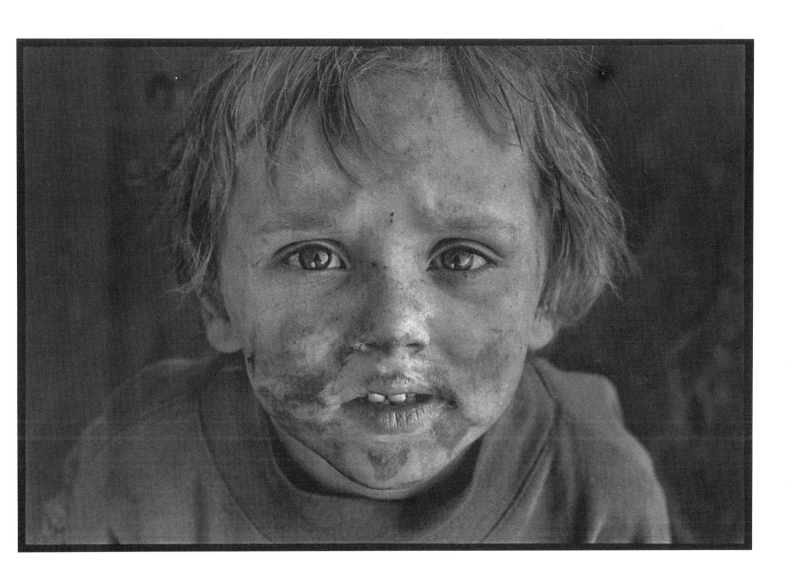

37

Trouble came to the homeless living on the east bank of the
Sacramento River in the spring of 1989, when Sacramento police warned they
could not camp in the woods along the shore. Blackie was living on
that side of the river when notices were put up telling campers they had to leave.

38

The Sacramento police sweep of the homeless.

39

Couple with a warning notice given during the Sacramento sweep.

40

Sacramento police inspected a homeless man's belongings.

41

Bridge underpass, Sacramento sweep.

42

City workers dismantled a homeless camp, Sacramento.
After the sweep, Blackie fled to West Sacramento,
a different legal jurisdiction in another county
across the Sacramento River. He built his house that summer.

43

Antihomeless sentiment was strong in Sacramento.

44

Because of the ever-increasing numbers of homeless on the west bank,
caused in part by the exodus from the police sweeps to the east
across the river, there were rumors that West Sacramento police would also make
a sweep. The morning of the west bank sweep, December 1989.

45

West Sacramento police on the shore.

46

Blackie watched for police the morning of the rumored sweep.
Blackie, along with Shorty and his partner Woody, decided not to leave,
but get citations and fight in court for the right to keep their camp.
They were tired of running and had nowhere to hide from police—
fourteen California cities at that time were sweeping the homeless,
as were cities in many other states.

47

West Sacramento police led the media on the
homeless sweep on the shore near Blackie's house.

48

Television camera operators filmed a campfire.

49

*A West Sacramento police officer doused a fire with coffee
that had been brewing on a grill. The camp's
occupants fled moments before when they saw police coming.*

50

West Sacramento police inspected the belongings
of residents living on the shore.

51

A couple routed from their camp by West Sacramento police.

52

A West Sacramento police officer looked for needle track marks

on a homeless man, who came out clean.

53

People caught up in the police sweep.

54

Shorty was cited for "maintaining a public nuisance" while a second officer checked for any outstanding warrants against him.

55

Woody being cited by police.

56
Blackie being cited by police.

57
Blackie after police left the camp.

58

Tie-Tie, one of Blackie's dogs.

59

Tie-Tie's grave, after the dog was hit by a car just before
the sweep; Blackie held the dog as it died.

60

Notice to appear in court.

WEST SACRAMENTO POLICE DEPARTMENT

Nº 13976

NOTICE TO APPEAR ☐ TRAFFIC ☒ OTHER

DATE 15 DEC 19 89 TIME 0835 HRS DAY OF WEEK M T W T F S S

NAME (First, Middle, Last)
MICHAEL G DURANT

ADDRESS
TRANSIENT

CITY STATE ZIP CODE

DRIVER'S LICENSE NO. STATE CLASS BIRTH DATE 10-6-14 JUV. ☐

SEX M HAIR GRY EYES BLU HEIGHT 54 WEIGHT 150 RACE CAUC

VEHICLE LICENSE NO. STATE PASSENGERS M F

YEAR OF VEH. MAKE MODEL BODY STYLE COLOR

REGISTERED OWNER OR LESSEE ☐ SAME AS ABOVE

ADDRESS OF OWNER OR LESSEE ☐ SAME AS ABOVE

ITEMS CHECKED ARE CITED IN ACCORDANCE WITH 40610(b) CVC - See reverse
BOOKING REQUIRED ☒ CASE NO. 89-11092

VIOLATION(S)	CODE	SECTION	DESCRIPTION
☒ 373 (a)		MAINTAINING A PUBLIC
☐ NUISIANCE			
☐			
☐			
☐ 27315 ( ) VC NON-USE OF SEATBELT			

INSURANCE

SPEED				RADAR	CITY OF OCCUR
APPROX.	PF/Max	VEH. LMT	SAFE		

LOCATION OF VIOLATION(S)
ON APPROX. ½ SOUTH OF THE TOWER
BRIDGE
☐ OFFENSE(S) NOT COMMITTED IN MY PRESENCE, CERTIFIED ON INFORMATION AND BELIEF.

I CERTIFY UNDER PENALTY OF PERJURY THAT THE FOREGOING IS TRUE AND CORRECT.
EXECUTED ON THE DATE SHOWN ABOVE AT WEST SACRAMENTO CALIFORNIA

ISSUING OFFICER J RACENIS ID# P 102

NAME OF ARRESTING OFFICER, IF DIFFERENT FROM ABOVE ID#

WITHOUT ADMITTING GUILT, I PROMISE TO APPEAR AT THE TIME AND PLACE CHECKED BELOW.
X SIGNATURE

BEFORE A JUDGE OR A CLERK OF THE YOLO COUNTY MUNI COURT SYSTEM.
☐ TRAFFIC DIV. - 725 MAIN ST., RM. # 313 WOODLAND, CA 95695 666-8060
☒ DEPT. A - 906 SACRAMENTO AVE., WEST SACRAMENTO, CA 95605 372-2900
☐ WOODLAND - RM. # 111, 725 COURT ST WOODLAND, CA 95695 666-8050
☐ JUVENILE COURT

☒ DATE 16 JAN 1989 TIME 0830 AM

FORM APPROVED BY THE JUDICIAL COUNCIL OF CALIFORNIA
(5-7-8-88) V.C. 40500, 40513(b), 40522 P.C. 853.8

SEE REVERSE SIDE

61

Blackie outside the courtroom for his first appearance
with Woody and Shorty. The three men demanded a jury trial.
They hoped to use a necessity defense to convince
the jury to find them not guilty so they could keep the camp.

62

Because the men demanded a jury trial, it was left to the
next court appearance to start the process to determine if they were guilty
of maintaining a public nuisance by camping on the shore.
Thus, the men could continue living in the camp, at least until the next court date.
Blackie, surprised by the news, celebrated and hugged Vera,
a citizen who often visited the camp.

63

The men were unsure the afternoon they came back from court.
They had never challenged authority. Over the next several weeks,
they couldn't get through on the phone to talk with their
court-appointed attorney; they were unsure and apprehensive.

64

The men had to wait one month for the second court hearing.
They were anxious and bored. Shorty studied one of the magazines from
Blackie's collection. Blackie found the magazines in Dumpsters
and resold them to adult bookstores, but he kept the best for his library.

65

Shorty passed the time by playing with Mister, the hobo cat.

66

Many days and nights of drinking followed the first court appearance. Blackie took a drink one afternoon and this began a huge binge that included the dancing of the "Blackie jig."

67

The drinking as the second court date neared led to a fight one night,

after a campmate named Bill caused an explosion by throwing

a can of fuel into the fire. Blackie waking up in his

house the morning after the explosion, the worst night of the binge.

68

Blackie, Woody, and Shorty, the morning of the second court appearance.
They waited inside the bus belonging to Harry, another
homeless man who lived on the shore. Harry drove the men to the courthouse
located in an old store in a strip shopping center;
the city of West Sacramento could not afford a real courthouse.

69

Shorty made himself presentable for the judge
in the window of a Cadillac.

70

Shorty and Blackie checked in with the court clerk.

71

*Blackie waited for his case to be called, after learning the fight
to keep the camp would involve many months of legal wrangling
and a lot of uncertainty, with slight chance of success.*

72

Blackie, Shorty, and Woody plea-bargained their case,
after deciding to abandon the fight.
The judge gave the men one month to vacate the camp.

73

After the court appearance, Blackie muttered,
"What's a hobo supposed to do?" He rolled a cigarette.

74

Blackie outside the courtroom.

75

A day before the court-ordered eviction date, Blackie carried one of his
aluminum pots to the truck belonging to a citizen who was going to help him
and the other hobos haul their belongings to a recycler to be sold.

76

Luke and Shorty assembled everything of value the men
could sell for scrap before they moved on.

77

Some of the belongings the men collected
from their houses to take with them.

78

Luke, in preparation for his first real hobo trip, got a final inspection
from Shorty. Luke wanted to be Shorty's hobo partner, but Shorty had other plans.
Luke went alone on a six-day hobo trip to Oregon.

79

Shorty and Blackie near the rice mill with a paper bag filled with
$8.12 worth of fortified wine and beer, bought with the proceeds from selling
scrap from the camp, the afternoon before the court-ordered eviction.

80

Alice and Burt decided to burn their camp the night before
the eviction, rather than let the police destroy it.

81

As Alice and Burt burned their camp, Blackie sat alone and
quiet about twenty feet away, drinking the wine bought with the money
they got for the camp's aluminum pots and other belongings.

82

Blackie walked with Moose on the way to his camp
for one of the last times, near the trailer of Fanny, the prostitute.
Moose followed Blackie everywhere.

83

Blackie moved into the Stardust Motel at the end of the camp's existence, to stay with his hobo friends Road Dog and Helga, who paid for the room.

84

Blackie stayed at the Stardust Motel for several weeks,
watching television and reading the
papers with glasses he found in a Dumpster.

85

While Blackie lived in the Stardust, Moose often ran
away to visit the shore and the abandoned camp.

86

The side of Blackie's house after it was abandoned.

87

Luke continued visiting the camp, hoping it would revive after
the police heat died down; he brought food from his
Dumpster diving to feed the men who no longer lived there.

88

Luke, alone in Blackie's Camp, waiting for Blackie to return to take
him on a trip to the National Hobo Convention in Iowa.
Luke considered Blackie to be the father he would liked to have had.

89

A picture from better times, left on the wall of one of the camp's houses.

90

When unseen hands began savaging the camp after the eviction,
Shorty did something that violated the nonterritorial nature of a hobo—
he wrote a warning. Shorty continued coming to the camp late at night,
leaving at dawn. Like Luke, Shorty did not want the camp to end.

91

While officers of the West Sacramento Police Department
were never seen coming to enforce the order to tear down the camp,
someone left a comment next to Shorty's warning.

92

Blackie's Camp was quickly vandalized.

93

Several months after Blackie was evicted from his house.

94

Late summer after Blackie's eviction.

95

All that marked the community that once claimed
a home along the shore of the Sacramento River were numerous
warning signs, posted at each former campsite.

96

The trash pit behind the outhouse at Blackie's Camp,
on the hill leading down to the beach.

97

A continuing drought after Blackie's Camp was abandoned
caused the river to recede that first summer, revealing artifacts.

98

Artifact on the shore below the camp.

99

*The river below Blackie's Camp, nearly three years after the camp
ceased to exist: a newspaper box washed ashore, rusted skeletal springs
from the car seat the Murray boys liked to play on.*

100

A sign used in the search for Blackie, at the annual National Hobo Convention
in Britt, Iowa. Blackie usually went to the convention, even though it
had become more commercialized. He went to the convention that
summer after the West Sacramento police sweep, but then vanished.
No one was found who'd since seen him on the hobo circuit.

THE PLACE

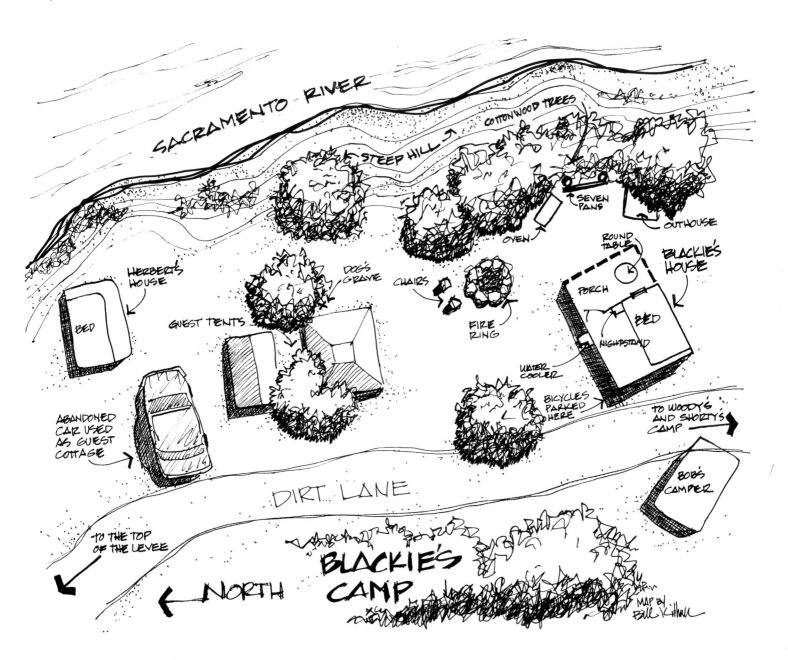

SACRAMENTO RIVER

STEEP HILL →

COTTONWOOD TREES

SEVEN PANS

OVEN

OUTHOUSE

ROUND TABLE

BLACKIE'S HOUSE

HERBERT'S HOUSE

DOG'S GRAVE

CHAIRS

PORCH

BED

NIGHTSTAND

BED

FIRE RING

WATER COOLER

GUEST TENTS

BICYCLES PARKED HERE

TO WOODY'S AND SHORTY'S CAMP

ABANDONED CAR USED AS GUEST COTTAGE →

BOB'S CAMPER

DIRT LANE

TO THE TOP OF THE LEVEE

← NORTH

BLACKIE'S CAMP

MAP BY Bill Kittu